Gangs II

Gangs II

ROSS KEMP

MICHAEL JOSEPH
an imprint of
PENGUIN BOOKS

MICHAEL JOSEPH
Published by the Penguin Group
Penguin Books Ltd, 80 Strand, London WC2R ORL, England
Penguin Group (USA) Inc., 375 Hudson Street, New York, New York 10014, USA
Penguin Group (Canada), 90 Eglinton Avenue East, Suite 700, Toronto, Ontario, Canada M4P 2Y3
(a division of Pearson Penguin Canada Inc.)
Penguin Ireland, 25 St Stephen's Green, Dublin 2, Ireland
(a division of Penguin Books Ltd)
Penguin Group (Australia), 250 Camberwell Road, Camberwell, Victoria 3124, Australia
(a division of Pearson Australia Group Pty Ltd)
Penguin Books India Pvt Ltd, 11 Community Centre, Panchsheel Park, New Delhi – 110 017, India
Penguin Group (NZ), 67 Apollo Drive, Rosedale, North Shore 0632, New Zealand
(a division of Pearson New Zealand Ltd)
Penguin Books (South Africa) (Pty) Ltd, 24 Sturdee Avenue, Rosebank, Johannesburg 2196, South Africa

Penguin Books Ltd, Registered Offices: 80 Strand, London WC2R ORL, England

www.penguin.com

First published 2008
1

Set in 13.5/16 pt Monotype Garamond
Typeset by Rowland Phototypesetting Ltd, Bury St Edmunds, Suffolk
Printed in Great Britain by Clays Ltd, St Ives plc

A CIP catalogue record for this book is available from the British Library

HARDBACK ISBN: 978-0-718-15441-7
TRADE PAPERBACK ISBN: 978-0-718-15479-0

www.greenpenguin.co.uk

Contents

Introduction   vii

1 Colombia   1

2 Poland   40

3 East Timor   75

4 LA   114

5 Kenya   166

6 Liverpool   209

Acknowledgements   240

Introduction

Over the past five years I have spent a lot of time away from home. Admittedly, with individuals most people would cross the road to avoid – in fact, anyone in their right mind would probably pay for a premium air fare to get away from them. I have seen poverty on a scale that most of us in the West will never experience. I have heard stories that still keep me awake at night and seen things that will stay with me for the rest of my life.

But not everything over those years has been doom and gloom. I think the crew and I developed an odd sense of humour, but then we were in some pretty odd situations, with some pretty odd people. As a result, there were some moments of great hilarity, when we would laugh and laugh at some particular incidents. When you spend your time investigating the gangs of the world, it pays to hold on to those instances. If I hadn't, I don't think I could have carried on making the programmes.

There was the time when Matt Bennett, the series producer, had to step in and direct the Los Angeles episode after the director was threatened to be killed by a Latino gang leader called Joker. (Believe me, Joker was no joke.) Joker had come up to me and said (these are his own words): 'If I see that mother fucker again, I am going to waste his arse on camera. And I ain't fuckin' wid ya.' Although at the time, I felt this would have made award-winning television, I had a small soft spot for this director and promptly suggested Matt take over.

The next night we met Joker and one of the smaller Latino gangs he controlled in Anaheim, South LA. As we rolled up to start filming, one of the younger gangsters pulled a Ruger pistol out of nowhere, stuck it through the window of the car and pointed it at me, asking 'what he could get me'. I suggested that we calm the situation down for a minute and got out of the car with the crew for a smoke break with our gangsters. In an attempt to bond Matt offered to put a fag in Joker's mouth, momentarily forgetting that the term 'fag' is used for someone who is gay in the US. After a brief silence, during which I held my breath, Joker just burst out laughing. 'Hey gay boy, you want to put something in my mouth?' At least it broke the ice and from then on Matt always religiously referred to them as cigarettes.

Our trip to Africa was longer than most in many ways. I have always been fascinated with this continent, the home of mankind. When we arrived, Kenya had just experienced some of the worst violence in its history, and the stories we were hearing were grim beyond belief: the desperation and poverty there were driving people to behave in unspeakably shocking ways. We were told about the Shit Squad, for example. These homeless orphaned kids live in the centre of Nairobi and frequent the few public conveniences there. To put food in their stomachs, they remove what doesn't get flushed away and cover their bodies in faeces. They then target wealthy people in the financial area of the city, with a rolled-up newspaper full of more faeces. If you don't hand over what they demand, you get newspaper and all. If you attempt to touch them, which I would advise against, you are not likely to get a grip anyway, you'll only receive more shit (quite literally).

Another street gang operating in Nairobi is the Iron Bar

Gang. One of them will approach you as you walk down the street and hit you full in the stomach. As your diaphragm collapses and air is expelled from your lungs, his cohort will come from behind with an iron bar shoved up his sleeve and hit you full across the oesophagus and put you in a neck lock. With no oxygen in your lungs and your airway blocked, it's not long before you pass out. Most victims not only wake up penniless, but also suffer the indignity of walking home naked and shoeless.

Luckily, Kenya offered us some moments of light relief. One incident that springs to mind happened when arriving late at a lodge once frequented by colonials. Tired from our eight-hour journey across rough terrain, all we really wanted was beer, food and sleep. As we walked into the bar, dusty and sweaty, we were confronted by some of the hardest faces I have ever seen. Black farmers from around the surrounding area came there on a Friday night to drink and eat and, well, let's put it this way, there were lots of 'ladies of the night' around. We weren't exactly made to feel welcome, and as we were off to a baptism which commenced at first light, we necked a quick beer and headed for bed. Taking my bag up to my room (if you can call it that), I first noticed that the door had been kicked from its hinges, rendering the key in my hand obsolete. As I switched the light on the bulb erupted, then blew. With the use of my head torch, which had taken me some five minutes to find in the dark, I searched around the room and found the bathroom, with the obligatory missing toilet seat, washed and climbed into bed. In these cases it's not wise to check the sheets. Needless to say they had a perfume all of their own and felt a little on the crusty side. I could already hear the whirring of mosquitoes above me. I looked through the mosquito net at them with my head torch. On closer inspection the net had holes big enough for humming birds to fly through, let alone mosquitoes. Having already succumbed to malaria once in my life, I sprayed myself in Deet, swallowed the anti-malarial tablet with a swig of water and turned the torch off. I was so tired that sleep came easily. I have no idea what length of time I slept for but it can only have been a matter of minutes.

Bang, bang, bang, bang. Heavy, high-heeled footsteps clattering up the stairs outside my room and along the corridor.

A sudden flurry of argumentative voices – a man and a woman – in a language I couldn't understand.

Zip, zip, clunk, clunk. The boots came off.

Jiggle, jiggle. The regular squeaking of a bed.

And then, suddenly, the sound of the man shouting in the throes of ecstasy while his partner yelled out what I can only imagine was a fake orgasm.

The business concluded, there was a brief pause before a tap started to run – clearly someone was washing some part of their anatomy, but it wasn't an image I really wanted to conjure.

Zip, zip, the boots went back on. Bang, bang, bang, bang, they hurried downstairs. More arguments as a price was presumably disputed. She started screaming at him, he started screaming at her.

Right, I thought to myself. I'm going to do something about this. But then I stopped. What could I possibly do? Wander out in my underwear to take on a prostitute and her john, miles from anywhere, and risk getting bitten even more? Much better to stick moistened rolled-up toilet paper in my ears and hope that the noise died down in time for me to grab at least an hour's shut-eye.

Finally, the argument reached some kind of resolution and the stillness of the African night once more descended upon my room.

But not for long . . .

I was just nodding off again when I heard a familiar sound.

Bang, bang, bang, bang.

Zip, zip, clunk, clunk.

Raised voices.

Jiggle, jiggle, squeak, squeak.

Moan, moan. Orgasm, 'orgasm'.

Silence. The running of a tap.

Zip, zip.

Bang, bang, bang, bang.

Shout, shout, shout.

By now I'm ready to weep. But I try to console myself. She's had two: surely a good night's work for anyone, or maybe not.

Mortgage rates must have gone up, maybe she owed money or maybe she just loved her job. Three more times it happened, by which stage I was almost able to conduct the proceedings like a maestro conducting an orchestra. It was one of the shortest, and yet somehow the longest, nights of my life. But we had a good laugh about it the next day.

I've met some fascinating people in the course of my investigations. People I liked, people I didn't, and people who I could never hope to fully understand. I've done my best to represent them fairly and honestly. I've tried not to gloss over the ugly parts, nor sensationalize what I've experienced. In short, I've attempted to tell the truth about what I've seen, the places I've gone to and the gangsters I've met. The result, I hope, is a taste of what it's really like to meet these violent, dangerous and unpredictable human beings. You'll see that it's a far cry from some of the music and films glamorizing the gangster way of life.

1. Colombia

If you know where to go, Colombia can be a tourist's paradise.

If you're the kind of guy who likes tall, sassy women, head for Medellin; if you like something a bit more curvaceous, Cartagena on the Caribbean coast is the place for you. Elsewhere there are modern cities with impressive skyscrapers; there are beautiful port towns; there are chic cobbled streets and old buildings bright with bougainvillea. You could go to Colombia on holiday and have a wonderful time. You could hit the beach; you could go dancing; you could shop till you dropped.

Or you could do what I did, and meet violent killers – men who can see to it that a life is extinguished for a handful of crumpled pesos. Because Colombia is home to the Paramilitaries, a 32,000-strong gang of vigilantes determined to take a unique brand of justice into their own hands.

For nearly half a century Colombia has been a country at war with itself. In the 1960s anti-government guerrillas such as the 18,000-strong Revolutionary Armed Forces of Colombia, or FARC, started to terrorize the civilian population as they attempted to spread their Marxist ideals. In the 1980s an illegal paramilitary army emerged to help the police and the military suppress these violent guerrilla groups. The Paramilitaries operated outside the law, but they had the silent approval of government officials. It was their self-imposed task to clean the streets of rogue elements, and they went about it with a swift, forceful efficiency. Of course, this was a recipe for chaos, and needless to say things soon got out of hand. Over time it became clear that the Paramilitaries were not quite the liberating force they claimed to be.

Both the guerrilla rebels and the Paramilitaries soon morphed into criminal organizations, and in Colombia, as in so many other parts of the world, there's only one way for criminal gangs to fund themselves: drugs. It is estimated that Colombia supplies 90 per cent of the cocaine that finds its way into the United States. *Coca* is big business, and it's not going away.

My principal destination on my trip to Colombia was the town of Medellin in the north, infamous for being the control centre of one of the most notorious drug barons of recent times: Pablo Escobar. Using the well-worn techniques of fear, intimidation and murder, Escobar controlled Medellin. Any judge, journalist or politician who spoke out against him was instantly removed. In order to keep his grip on the town, he needed a gang of killers – mercenary assassins, guns for hire. They were known as the *sicarios*. Escobar trained them up. He gave them guns. Pretty soon the *sicarios* became the ruthless force he needed them to be and very good at their job.

Pablo Escobar was killed in 1993, shot by government forces. Four years before his death he had been named the world's seventh-richest man. His Medellin cartel was earning US$30 billion a year and supplied 80 per cent of the world's cocaine. Escobar's death was never going to bring an end to his empire, however. Killing him was like cutting the head off a hydra: another was bound to grow in its place. The cartel was taken over by the United Self Defence Forces, or AUC – the largest illegal paramilitary army in the country. The AUC continued to use the *sicario* gangs to do their dirty work.

Escobar might have been out of the equation, but the violence didn't stop, and the demand for *coca* was still there. The killing continued, as bad as ever, if not worse. The Paramilitaries continued to insist that their role was to cleanse the streets of criminals and scum, but anyone with half a brain knew the truth was more complex than that.

In 2003 Colombia's President Uribe started a peace process. He offered the Paramilitaries an amnesty: if they laid down their weapons and demobilized, they would be offered full pardon for all crimes committed in the past. The initiative was approved by leaders around the world, and on the surface it looked like a success. Guns were handed in; high-level Paramilitaries denounced their way of life. But the word on the street is that the amnesty is not all it seems to be. It is said that some of the Paramilitary gangs are very far from disarmed, and we had heard rumours that *sicario* assassins were operating just as ruthlessly – and effectively – as ever.

So it was that when I arrived in Colombia my intentions were these: to speak to the Paramilitaries; to ask them face to face if they have truly demobilized; to try and understand why they continue to bring terror to the streets. I also wanted to track down a *sicario*. And I wanted to speak to some of the victims of the gang warfare that has turned Colombia into one of the most violent countries in the world.

It wasn't going to be straightforward. Medellin, as I was soon to find out, was a place plagued with paranoia, a place where only the bravest – or the most reckless – were prepared to speak. And the Paramilitary gangs, of course, weren't even supposed to exist.

It was clear to me, even before I started, that there was more to Colombia than the tourist brochures suggested.

*

It was getting dark, and it had been a long day. But I had learned a lot about life in Colombia in the last few hours.

I had nearly been killed in the morning, not by the Para-militaries or FARC guerrillas, but by the wing mirror of a taxi. Medellin is situated in a vast volcanic punchbowl. Around the edges are hills covered with districts – or *communas* – and intricate mazes of roads with unbelievably steep inclines. To save petrol, taxi drivers switch off their engines and coast down these streets at breakneck speed without a thought for what might be round the next corner. On that morning it was *me* round the next corner. A couple of inches to the left and my quest to track down the Paramilitaries would have been brought to an abrupt – and permanent – halt.

This wasn't the only vehicle-based trauma we had to put up with while we were there. Our white Nissan van had been supplied by some local fixers who seemed very proud of their vehicle, but in truth, it was a total liability. It broke down several times during our trip and had a particularly complicated immobilizing system. You had to press a button down by the handbrake and then another button on the key ring in order to get out of the van without immobilizing it. It also had difficulty going uphill – a bit of a problem if you are driving round a town built on some of the steepest gradients I'd ever seen – and had a habit of breaking down when you went downhill. And of course I was always for-getting the immobilizing procedure, meaning I would find myself locked out of it on a pretty regular basis.

We'd had all kinds of difficulty with the van that morning, and around midday we had a funeral to attend. I had met the group of women who called themselves the Mothers of Candelaria earlier in our stay. Every Wednesday they meet outside a church in Medellin to hold a kind of demonstration or vigil. They have all lost friends or family who they believe to have been kidnapped or killed by Paramilitaries or FARC guerrillas. That first meeting with them had been deeply moving. I had interviewed a woman named Aura, who just three months ago had been waiting for her father to return to their home in the slums – or *barrios* – and wish her a happy birthday. He never arrived. Word reached her that he had been abducted in FARC territory, but Aura had no idea whether he had been killed or just kidnapped. She had no idea whether she would ever see him again. She had lost her husband the same way some years earlier. The moment I met her, I could see the grief in the woman's face. I could hear it in her voice.

I had also heard about a woman called Judith Vergara. Judith was a community worker from a district of Medellin known as Communa 13. The previous year she had openly tried to stop the Paramilitaries moving into her neighbourhood to recruit. She had been approaching the young people of the area, telling them to resist the advances of the Paramilitaries, to ignore them when they came to call. Judith was kidnapped and told to stop interfering, but as a mother, unable to stand the vicious circle of violence she saw all around her, she refused.

I had arranged to meet her, to talk to her and hear what she had to say. But things have a way of going terribly wrong in situations like this. Just the previous day Judith had paid the ultimate price for standing up to the Paramilitaries. She had been travelling to work on a bus when she was approached by two men with guns. They shot her in the head at point-blank range. She died instantly. Judith Vergara was thirty-two years old. And now, instead of interviewing her, I was going to her wake.

You could hear the wails even as you approached the small chapel where the service was being held. Hollow, inhuman shrieks of grief. Once inside, you could almost touch the sadness. And yet there was something else in the air as well. A sense of acceptance. I suppose that if you live in a country where 35,000 people have disappeared in ten years, death becomes a way of life. Judith knew what she was getting into. She knew the risks she was running. That didn't make it any easier, though, to see her four children and her husband weeping over her open casket.

I looked at her body myself. She had been shot in the face and chest, but there was no sign of it: the morticians in Colombia are very skilled at their work. After all, they have plenty of chances to practise. She was barefoot, but otherwise plainly clothed. She looked very small in death, and it was brought home to me that this one woman was hardly a match for the might of the Paramilitaries. It just went to show how determined certain people were in this county to eliminate anyone who opposed them.

I didn't stay there long; I couldn't bear to. When I left, I felt as though I had intruded upon someone else's grief. Walking out emotionally exhausted, I slumped against the wall and tried to compose myself. Suddenly there was someone in front of me – a woman from the chapel. She spoke no English; I spoke no Spanish. But as I sat there, she took my hands in hers and stayed with me for perhaps fifteen minutes. I was struck by the warmth of this woman, a warmth that I saw repeated in so many people in so many places throughout my stay – despite the fact that they were surrounded by so much death and violence.

Not everyone, however, was quite that compassionate, as I was to discover later in the day.

By the time we left the chapel we were all in need of

something to eat. John the director and I piled into the cursed white Nissan and we drove off in convoy with the rest of the crew to find some food. By this time I had removed the immobilizing button from the key ring, and John was sitting in the passenger seat fiddling with it.

'Don't play with that, John,' I warned as I struggled round a roundabout in the mid-afternoon traffic.

As I spoke, there was a click. John had pressed the button. Instantly the steering wheel locked. So did the doors.

Traffic was coming at us from all sides; cars beeped their horns at the white van with the stupid gringo who couldn't control his vehicle. I shouted a few words I wouldn't want my mum to hear as I clenched my muscles and coasted off the roundabout and into a nearby parking spot, lucky that I hadn't just become the main player in a big pile-up. The only way we could exit the car was by climbing out of the tailgate. We didn't have a mobile phone with us, and it took three and a half hours for the others to locate us.

All in all, the day was not panning out quite how we had intended. But there was a schedule to stick to, so once we had eaten and the van had been seen to, we carried on with the day's filming.

In a place like Medellin local knowledge is everything. You can't just call on a holiday rep if you're trying to set up a meeting with a trained killer, so your local knowledge has to come from a more unconventional source. Towards evening we met up with one of our Colombian fixers, a man to whom I took an almost instant dislike. He was a plump guy, stocky and thickset. It was difficult to judge how old he was – perhaps in his thirties. He had a constant smile on his face – no doubt helped by the fact that he was perpetually smoking a spliff like some people chain-smoke cigarettes, and frequently disappeared to feed his cocaine habit as well

– but you could tell it was a smile that was hiding something. He was scrupulously friendly, but he had the eyes of a killer. He also had eyes for Marta, our assistant producer. She said our man gave her the creeps – something all the crew were in agreement with.

Our fixer told us that he could set us up with a *sicario* assassin. It was only later that I found out how he was able to do that – this guy was a kind of agent, a broker between the Paramilitaries and the *sicario*. If you want the streets cleansed of a particular person, you come to this guy and he arranges it – for a price. At the time I didn't ask too many questions.

Our fixer took us to the outskirts of Medellin, high above the city, but by the time we got there it was too dark to film anything other than a cutaway of the lights illuminating all across the punchbowl. It had been an exhausting day, and all I wanted to do was get back to my hotel for a bath and beer. I was driving a white Toyota Land Cruiser, but I didn't know the way back, so I accepted an offer from the fixer to guide me back down into Medellin.

Leaving the camera crew, we headed off. He was already slurring his words when he got into the car, high on weed and coke, smiling and laughing at nothing in particular. He would shout directions at me in Spanish as I tried to weave my way back down into the punchbowl, going from village to village as we tacked down the hillside tiers that make up the suburbs of the city. As I drove, I couldn't help noticing that people would look at us in alarm, then suddenly disappear. I couldn't work it out at first, but the penny soon dropped: I was driving a white four-by-four, just like the Paramilitaries; I had a shaved head, just like the Paramilitaries; and the guy in the seat next to me, off his face on God knows what, was a *sicario* agent. I started to

8

feel pretty uncomfortable. How a bloke from Essex can end up looking like a Colombian Paramilitary, I don't know. But apparently I do.

None of this seemed to worry my guide. He was laughing away like he didn't have a care in the world. He didn't even seem too worried when we were pulled over by a squad of military policemen manning one of the impromptu road-blocks that had been recently set up, ostensibly to catch Judith Vergara's killer.

Shit, I thought. This was all I needed.

I knew the fixer was carrying drugs; whether he was carrying a weapon or not was anybody's guess. There was a babble of voices from the cops; the fixer climbed out of the vehicle and put his hands up against its sides and he and the cops started to talk in animated Spanish. I didn't have a clue what any of them were saying. Meanwhile, I'm still sitting behind the wheel, wondering what the hell I should be doing. I fully expected the cops to find my guide's stash, and even if I spoke the language it would have been difficult for me to explain what I was doing with him. I sensed that my next stop might be the inside of a Colombian jail cell. Not quite what I had in mind.

The police gestured at me to get out. Like the fixer, I put my hands up against the side of the truck. In an instant I had four guns pointing in my direction – Colombian versions of the AK-47. All around me I can hear nothing but voices chattering in Spanish, when suddenly I feel myself being patted down. There's a hand on my chest, and to my surprise it gives me a good squeeze, like a grope, followed by a hearty laugh and more animated Spanish. Whenever I'm away, I always carry my passport with me. I slowly put my hand into my pocket and pulled it out, but they weren't interested in it, so back it went as they continued to pat me down. I felt a hand on my leg; it made its way round to my inner thigh.

And then, from nowhere, a short, sharp blow, right into my bollocks.

I gasped, and my nails dug into the paintwork of the car as tears sprang to my eyes. The police had a good old laugh – clearly it had been part of the plan to give the gringo a bit of a tap. It was only after a while that I realized that the whole purpose of this little display was to take the piss out of me. I was allowed back into the car, along with the fixer. Quite why he hadn't been taken off for possessing drugs, I don't know – maybe he was in cahoots with them, maybe they just didn't care – but while I drove away with swollen testicles, he carried on snorting more coke. This wasn't party time for him – he was snorting lines from the groove of a key like some people smoke cigarettes. All the while he was laughing about what had just happened to me. It was a big joke to him, but you never quite get used to having a gun pointed in your direction, and there's nothing like a karate chop in the *cojones* to dampen your sense of humour . . .

After a couple of hours we made it down into the punchbowl, and I agreed to take the fixer back to his *communa*. As we entered the district, he kept telling me that he controlled it, that it was his. He was proud of this fact. Boastful. I didn't know quite what he meant. Perhaps he was 'cleaning it up' for the Paramilitaries; maybe he was taking a cut of all the drug deals going down here. Maybe he was just bigging himself up for my benefit. Whatever it was, whatever he was doing here, his input was clearly doing very little to improve the area.

It was like Dante's inferno, a wasteland of misery that looked like the aftermath of some horrific nuclear accident. Although it was dark outside, I could still see the people on the side of the road. They were like wraiths. Clearly they were drug addicts – crack, most likely, as cocaine would have been too expensive for people like this. There were men and women with their teeth knocked out and terrible cuts and sores on their faces. Many of them were semi-naked, wearing only rags black with soot and dirt. Their faces had helpless, desperate expressions, and they looked barely human, like a different species.

By the side of the road were gulleys, like small storm drains, a couple of metres in depth. They are just there to take the effluent and shit off the street. Looking carefully, I saw people lying in them, it was a hot night, so maybe it was a way of cooling off, but they had covered areas with straw or plastic bags and had made little dwellings – permanent ones – in the fetid gutter.

Young and old, the place was littered with junkies and prostitutes. Glue-abuse kids, crack whores – it was like something out of a zombie film. Bodies lay over each other: you could only tell they were alive when a limb occasionally moved. Ours was the only car in the area, and everyone looked at it with hungry curiosity. I got the impression that if I hadn't been with the fixer, they'd have been clambering over the car trying to break in. There was no doubt in my mind that the fixer had brought me here in order to shock me; if that was the case, he certainly succeeded. I knew he was a crook, but if I had known that he presided over such a place, that he actively encouraged these people to become drug addicts and then took money from the Paramilitaries to remove them from the streets, I would never have had anything to do with him. He was truly one of life's scumbags.

I couldn't get out of there quickly enough. I dumped the fixer, hoping I'd never have to see him again, and floored it back towards my hotel. But as I left the *communa*, I realized that I was about to run out of petrol, and I had no money on me. I cursed: there was no way I was going to be able to get back to the hotel, and I certainly didn't want to be stranded in downtown Medellin after the sight I had just seen, and knowing what I now knew about the place. When I saw a petrol station, I pulled over and left them my watch in exchange for a tank of gas, promising to come back with some money later. I got back to the hotel, picked up some cash, returned to the petrol station, paid them, and drove back to the hotel again.

It had been just another day filming *Gangs*, but an eye-opening one. I wanted a beer but the bar was closed, so I bathed and then went to bed. I tried to sleep, but unsuccessfully as images of what I had just seen bounced around in my head. As I lay in my relatively clean sheets, head on my relatively clean pillow, I couldn't get it out of my head that there were people not so far away having a very different kind of night. A worse one. It was an uncomfortable thought, and an uncomfortable night.

It was a journalist in Medellin who finally gave us the name of a *sicario* who might be willing to talk, and a meeting was set up in the area where the assassin lived – Barrio Popular, way up in the hills out of town. The journalist himself refused to come with us. He said it was too dangerous. From what I had learned about this city, I was beginning to think he might be right.

Our *sicario* was young, just twenty-five. They are trained to be assassins from a very young age, because you're much less likely to expect a child to pull a gun on you, and our man was ten years old when he first started working for the Paramilitaries. A pretty sobering notion, especially when I thought back to what I was like as a ten-year-old.

It was early in the morning as I drove the white Nissan round the winding maze of streets that led to Barrio Popular. I'd been given vague directions – we were to meet by a shrine to the Virgin Mary, of which there are many hundreds in this deeply Catholic country – but I didn't really know where I was going, which only added to the sense of apprehension. When we finally found the rendezvous point, we had to wait for quite a while – these gangsters don't really do early in the morning – and I could sense the curiosity and the threatening glances of the people around. They were obviously wondering what the hell a camera crew was doing on their turf. Medellin is a paranoid place, and we were just adding to the atmosphere of suspicion.

Our *sicario*'s name was Andres. It's difficult to say what his motivation was for speaking to us – fame, most likely – but he had asked for one thing: a football shirt with the name of one of Colombia's most famous exports emblazoned on the back – Juan Pablo Angel, formerly of Aston Villa and now plying his trade in the US Major League. The football shirt had gone on before us, and it was odd to see Andres saunter up the steep road proudly wearing his Villa strip. He was already stoned, but that was to be expected in this part of town. We shook hands and he led me away from the meeting place towards the little house where he lived.

It wasn't his house; it belonged to a woman known as the 'old witch'. She was elderly, gap-toothed but smiling, and with a sharp, wise look in her eyes. The crone was friendly, but in a knowing kind of way – there was no doubt in my mind that she was deeply dodgy. There were perhaps twelve or thirteen people living in her little house – criminals, pickpockets, assassins. She was Colombia's female version of Fagin, and obviously ruled the roost. When she saw the Thermos flask I had with me, she kept pointing at it and nodding. At first I thought she wanted a cup of coffee, but then I realized it was the Thermos itself she was after. It was an object of value, I guess, and this woman wasn't stupid. I handed it over. It was clearly the right thing to do.

Andres explained to us when we arrived that he used to run with her son. When her boy was shot dead, the old witch took Andres under her wing. His own mother was still alive, and they still saw each other, but she had no idea of the path her son had taken. As far as she was concerned, he was a lovely, hard-working boy. I didn't know if he lived in this place all the time, but he certainly seemed at home here.

He took us up the thin, winding flight of steps that led to his room, and as he did so I was struck by the powerful smell of poverty. It's a smell you get all over the world – a foul mixture of boiled cabbage (even though there's seldom any cabbage to boil), cheap meat that smells like dog food being cooked and human excrement – hardly surprising in a place where shit runs out into the streets and people take a piss on the pavement. Somewhere in the mix there's also the strong, heady smell of marijuana, and the odour of damp coming from the cheaply constructed buildings.

Andres's room was tiny, like a little cell – it even had bars across the tiny window. It was no bigger than two metres by five – quite cramped for me, him and a camera crew. The walls were made out of some kind of muddy brick, and there was a single electric light hanging from the ceiling. There were pictures on the wall and personal items dotted around – an attempt to personalize the place – but it looked more like a cave than a home.

It was ten o'clock in the morning by now, and Andres had already smoked a lot of dope. He was very proud of how good his dope was, and I could tell he wasn't lying. I'm particularly susceptible to marijuana, and I have to be wary of people smoking it around me, especially in enclosed spaces, or the interview suffers. The clouds he was puffing out of his nose were already making me feel intoxicated, but it wasn't like I could just ask him to put out his spliff. This was a place were you could buy joints already rolled and wrapped in cellophane. He continued to smoke all the time we were there.

Andres was one of the Paramilitaries' top assassins, and he used to be on the government's most wanted list. Since demobilization, however, he has received a pardon. I didn't know if he was still active, and I couldn't simply come straight out and ask him. All I could do was listen to what he had to say, and try to understand the life of a *sicario*.

The assassin in front of me was unable to say how many men he had killed. He simply couldn't remember, not least because he was almost always on drugs when he worked. What he could remember, though, was the first time he had killed someone, when he was just ten years old. I guess that's not the kind of thing anyone would forget very easily. Certainly his description of that moment was the kind of thing that stays with you. 'Back then you had to prove yourself to the gang,' he told me. 'It was like, "Come here, you, you have to prove you are a man." For me it was the most shocking thing. Seeing that person gasping for breath was traumatizing. I wasn't even able to walk afterwards, and everything smelt of blood. A trauma. The nightmares would wake me up. The nightmares only stopped when I did it again. It started to become part of my life, part of the world that I was in.'

As Andres smoked more dope he became less lucid, but he did manage to explain to me that after a while killing becomes like a drug itself. If you go for a few days without a fix, you start to feel the need for the adrenalin rush once more. 'You need to feel the vertigo from it,' he told me. 'Do you understand? Feel the vertigo . . .'

I was to spend a lot more time with Andres during my stay and soon I began to understand him a bit better. He fancied himself as a bit of a ladykiller – in more ways than one – and was a good-looking lad with a twinkle in his eye. Andres had no shortage of girlfriends – his own little harem. Some of them were pregnant, and there was a fair sprinkling of children dotted around. This was hardly a surprise to me, because it was a situation I had seen repeated around the world. So often, you meet guys who join a gang wanting to be the toughest boy on the block because that's attractive to women. If they're not going to be Juan Pablo Angel and play football for their country, they may decide they're going to become a gangster and attract women that way.

Andres explained to me that he employed two main methods to kill his victims: the gun and the knife. Killing someone, though, is easy, he told me; it's getting away with it that's the difficult bit, and in Medellin the *sicarios* had come up with a novel way of pulling off their hits. Andres took me down into the centre of the city to explain how it worked.

Several years ago a law was passed in Colombia making it mandatory for all motorbike riders to display the registration number of their bikes on the back of specially made jackets and helmets. This was because the *sicarios* were carrying out their assassinations by bike. There would generally be two of them – a driver and a shooter – and they would cover the registration number of the bike before they set off. The *sicarios* would locate their victim, and then follow them until they were somewhere with a clear shot. 'You wouldn't do it somewhere difficult,' Andres explained. 'You would look for a place where it was easier to escape and where there weren't too many police or grasses.' Hence the law forcing people to display their registration number on their clothes. But it's not exactly foolproof – you can just steal someone else's jacket for a start, or make one up of your own, as the jackets are available anywhere.

I learned from Andres some of the *sicarios'* techniques for carrying out a hit on someone in a car. Sometimes they hit people when the vehicle is moving, but generally not if they are going after the driver. Put a bullet in the head of somebody in charge of a moving car, the vehicle will go out of control, and the assassins risk getting caught up in the crash that will inevitably follow. Most hits, therefore, are carried out on a stationary car, and as the traffic in Medellin is so appalling, the motorbike will be long gone down some winding street before the police or emergency services arrive on the scene. The same technique is used for armed robberies: you pull up beside someone, put a gun through their window and demand their purse or wallet. Before the victim knows it, the motorbike has disappeared. It's a pretty effective way to do business.

Andres and I got on well. I think he sensed I wasn't there to judge him but was happy for him just to say his piece. The more time we spent together that day, the more he opened up, and although he was still vigilant about what he said, I felt that I was getting to know him increasingly well. The moment came when I felt I could ask him whether he was still operating as a *sicario*.

The answer came back loud and clear: 'No.'

But I wasn't so sure. Andres was getting his money from somewhere, and though I was pretty confident he was dealing drugs on the side, I had the impression that wasn't the end of the story. Moreover, I wondered how someone who had been a killer for all his adult life, and much of his childhood too, could simply put that way of life to one side.

All things considered, it would be astonishing if he really had gone straight. But Andres knew full well that if he admitted to any new killings since his pardon, he'd go straight to prison.

I asked him if he would put me in touch with one of his ex-bosses. After all, if the Paramilitaries had decommissioned, there was no reason for them not to talk to me.

Again, the answer was firm: 'No.'

It looked like if I was going to get any further access to the Paramilitaries, if I was going to get anyone in the know to admit that the *sicario* gangs were still active, I wouldn't be doing it through Andres. I was going to have to find a different way in.

The demobilization of the Paramilitaries caused a logistical and social problem for the Colombian authorities. You have tens of thousands of people who have known nothing throughout their entire lives but brutal warfare and suddenly you give them a pardon on the basis that they will not return to that way of life. The question is, what way of life *do* they return to? The government realized that they needed to address this problem, and so set up vast schools where former Paramilitaries could go to be trained in anything from maths to plumbing to business studies. My next trip was to one of these schools.

There's something a bit unnerving about being surrounded by 5,000 former Paramilitaries, but that was the situation I found myself in. I was escorted into a classroom by two ex-Paramilitary officers called Montoya and Joaquim. The students had been told that I was here just to see what a Paramilitary school looks like, to witness the good work that was being done. But the moment I walked into the classroom where we were to film, it was clear from the atmosphere that nobody believed us. Everyone knew we had an agenda; everyone seemed to know we were there to try and find out if the Paramilitaries had really thrown down their arms or not. I wondered what kind of response I was going to get to my questions.

I looked round the class and I asked Montoya if everyone here had been a Paramilitary at one point.

'Affirmative. They were all members of the Paramilitary force.'

I glanced at the people in the room with me. There weren't just men in the class; perhaps one in five of them were women. I had heard that both FARC and the Paramilitaries had women working for them, who were notorious for being some of the hardest and most brutal killers around. And for assassinations women are very handy. If you're standing at a bus stop, you're a lot less likely to expect some pretty woman to pull a gun on you than some hulking guy in a mask. And scenarios like that are more common than you might think. If I've learned anything from meeting gangs around the world, it is this: if you're brutalized, then you'll behave in a brutal manner. If your husband and children have been wiped out by the Paramilitaries, you'll join FARC whether you're forced into it or not; if FARC have done you wrong, the Paramilitaries can count on your support. You want blood back for the blood that's been spilled. If someone's killed your husband and destroyed your life, you want revenge. Seeing the women in that classroom was a striking reminder of the realities of the Colombian situation.

I asked Montoya if he found it difficult to go from carrying a gun every day to advocating peace.

'When I realized that crime doesn't pay,' he replied, 'I made an effort and changed completely, and now I work with the community.' But were people still scared of him in the *barrios*? 'There might be a few people who are a bit reluctant to accept this change we've embarked on, but most of the community supports us. We have been building respect with them, not based on guns but based on trust.'

His words sounded plausible and well meant. But they also sounded slightly rehearsed, and it hadn't escaped my notice that in the room there were a couple of older guys who the others seemed to be somewhat wary of. They just sat there not saying much, but it was clear to me that they were there to keep tabs on what was said. With them in the room nobody was going to put a foot wrong. Nobody was going to answer my questions truthfully – they were just going to say what the Paramilitaries wanted me to hear.

'The majority of people I've spoken to since I've come to Medellin seem very happy about the demobilization,' I commented. 'There are a few people I've spoken to that have said some of the Paramilitaries haven't demobilized. Is that true?'

Montoya's answer was predictable. 'Here we definitely have a very serious peace process. There may be some, but this is not confirmed in other areas outside Medellin. But definitely here in Medellin the whole of the organic structure got demobilized. There aren't any new groups of Para-militaries.'

I didn't believe him, but there was no way I was going to argue. These guys knew where I was staying, and they no doubt had connections with some pretty violent people. And yet, despite the fact that I was being stonewalled whenever I tried to get to the truth about demobilization, I didn't come away from the school with the impression that the men and women there were just going through the motions. Everyone there had been denied an education when they were children; none of them had been given the skills they needed to make an honest living. Even if some of them hadn't demobilized, educating them was undoubtedly a step in the right direction. I asked the class how many of them had lost close family as a direct result of the conflict between the Paramilitaries and the guerrillas. Out of a class of forty, about thirty-six put up their hands. It was a telling statistic, and I left the school hoping that education would do something to help these people whose lives had been ravaged by violence.

I had met an ex-*sicario*. I had met former Paramilitaries who had supposedly thrown down their guns. But so far I had not met anyone willing to confirm what everyone suspected: that for a certain hard core of Paramilitaries demobilization was a myth. Whenever I got close, it seemed that people were too scared to talk, and having seen Judith Vergara's body laid out in her coffin, it wasn't difficult to understand why.

The closest I had got was with Andres. He had killed for a living, and we seemed to have some sort of rapport. He'd agreed to meet me again, but this time at a very different place to the old witch's house.

The Church of Our Lady of the Rosary in Medellin is an impressive, imposing and beautiful place. In many ways the very existence of this church in modern-day Medellin is a symbol of the deep social divide that exists in Colombia. It's a magnificent building, encrusted with gold and full of rich artwork depicting glorious moments in the country's history. And yet, only metres away, you see the poverty. You see the beggars and the street kids, like something out of a novel by Charles Dickens. You see the filth, the crime and the despair. Children trawl through bins, their faces and hands covered in glue from solvent abuse, and if you're eating something on the street, they will follow you and ask for some. Where extreme poverty and relative affluence exist side by side, violence is only to be expected.

What is perhaps not to be expected is the religious doubt of a hired killer.

The Church of Our Lady of the Rosary was a good hour away from where Andres lived, which made it slightly surprising that this was where he wanted to hook up with us. As always, it wasn't a straightforward meet. We had to tell the priest at the church that we were here to film a documentary about the building itself. I felt bad about lying to a priest, but consoled myself that we'd done it in a nice way. Had he known our true purpose, he would never have let us through the front door. The priest was fully aware that this was a place where *sicarios* come, and it wasn't something he'd want to publicize to the world at large.

There was something weird about walking on holy ground with a man who had been murdering people since the age of ten, but I don't think Andres saw it that way. Still wearing his Angel football shirt – the irony of which was not lost on me – he seemed perfectly at home here. Against one of the walls of this beautiful church was a statue of the Madonna. This, Andres explained to me, was Mary the Helper. She helps the unprotected, and it is to this very Madonna that the *sicarios* would come to pray for protection before they went out on an assassination job.

'I'd pray for protection,' Andres explained to me. 'For nothing bad to happen to me. Just in case anything went wrong. For us, she's like a mother. And I don't think a mother passes judgement. It must be hard for her to see us like that, a little crazy. But I don't think she judges.'

As Andres spoke, and as he looked up at this patron saint of assassins, I sensed in him a conflict, a strange mixture of acceptance of his past and guilt at what he had done. I tried to understand what someone like this would gain from seeking solace in a church. At the end of the day, I suppose, everyone needs somebody to talk to, and that was the one thing Andres didn't have. He couldn't go to his real mother and confess what he had done, because his mother had no idea what he was into. He couldn't go to the other *sicarios* and vent his feelings because he'd just come over as a softie – or worse, a grass. And so he came here, seeking the acceptance that he couldn't get from anyone else, seeking comfort from someone who would offer him protection and never judge him, or tell on him. Religion is used as therapy by people all around the world, and if anybody needed a bit of therapy, it was the assassin standing in front of me.

It was not a great surprise, in such a deeply religious country as Colombia, that Andres should have some kind of religious conviction, but I couldn't help wondering, after all the things he had done, which way he thought he was going when his number was up: heavenwards or the other direction. I asked him if he thought God would forgive him for what he had done.

'I think that if I don't do it again he might forgive me, but not otherwise.'

It was a strange answer. Certainly it didn't sound like the kind of response to be expected from a man who had completely turned his back on killing. And what he said next only confirmed my doubts.

'I haven't told God that I won't do it again or made him any promises because it wouldn't be good to disappoint him ... I'm not promising; I'm just trying not to do it again. And trying to have the courage not to go back.'

But if there were no Paramilitaries employing *sicarios* to do their dirty work, why would going back to the grisly business of assassination even be an option for Andres?

I'm not promising; I'm just trying not to do it again.

He had spoken those words nonchalantly. Offhand. Like he was asking someone for a cigarette. And as I left the church with him and we said our goodbyes, I couldn't help thinking that it really wasn't much of a promise.

It had become clear to me during my stay in Colombia that no matter how much the likes of Andres and the guys and girls in the school liked to deny it, the truth was that the Paramilitaries were most definitely still active on the streets of Medellin. As if further proof were needed, I arranged to meet with Jorge Ceballos, a government official who specialized in investigating human rights abuses such as the murder of Judith Vergara.

Even before Jorge opened his mouth, it was obvious his belief that the Paramilitaries had not universally demobilized was hardly a figment of his imagination. We met in Communa 8, perhaps the most violent district in Medellin. Just prior to our visit twelve locals had been assassinated over a three-week period, and Jorge had insisted that we surround ourselves with bodyguards. There's nothing like an escort of men clad in body armour carrying military assault rifles and with Berettas stuffed down the back of their pants to remind you that the danger you've been warned of is very real indeed. This was no set-dressing: put a step wrong in this part of town and you end up dead.

Jorge Ceballos was one of God's children. A cheerful man, he chain-smoked red Marlboros and was loved by everyone he met. He drank the thick black Colombian coffee that I couldn't take – a fact that made him laugh at me good-naturedly. For a man who spends his life investigating brutal murders, he is incredibly upbeat. He probably will be until the day he gets shot, a day I can't help feeling isn't too far in the future. But Jorge commands respect and has a loyal following of people who treat him like others might a priest. It's easy to see why. He may not be from the same social class as the people who live in the poverty of Communa 8 and similar areas, but that doesn't stop him caring about them and for them. He's intelligent and careful, and he has the *cojones* openly to criticize the government.

As we walked through Communa 8, people came out of their houses to look at us. Immediately, Jorge was able to tell me if they were Paramilitaries or ex-Paramilitaries. He explained to me that while some Paramilitaries had indeed demobilized, there were still a significant number – how many, he couldn't say – who continued to commit crimes in the city and who have kept the Paramilitary structure and organization intact. They were not massacring people ten to fifteen at a time like they used to, but they were still killing them.

I asked Jorge why he thought the Paramilitaries haven't disarmed. He shrugged, then told me that they made money out of it. A lot of political organizations in Colombia with Paramilitary wings fund their activities through extortion and drugs. All of a sudden peace is imposed and their bosses are telling them to put their guns down. But they've been earning money through illicit means, and it's hard to stop. And if you want to carry on, you need strength in numbers. Half your allies have given up because they've been pardoned by the government – some of them have even been given jobs by the government – and so you need to keep recruiting young men and women from the streets. The more people you have, the more power you have; the more power you have, the more money you get. It always comes down to the green.

Jorge told me that if it wasn't for the fact that we were

surrounded by his heavily armed security guards, there was no way we'd have been able to walk and talk freely through these streets. I believed him. But I still wanted to speak to people closer to the active Paramilitaries. I wanted to hear the truth of their involvement in Colombia's street violence straight from the horse's mouth. So far, however, we had gone down a lot of dead-end roads.

Then, a couple of days later, we had a breakthrough. Someone was willing to talk to us. I didn't know it yet, but he turned out to be about as far removed from Jorge's benevolence as it's possible to be.

He insisted that his name be kept a secret, which hardly came as a surprise in this paranoid world of Colombian gangs. But he probably had more reason than most to keep his identity under wraps. Like the fixer who had proudly shown me the *communa* he ran, he was an agent for assassins. Say you don't like your husband any more and you want him killed, this guy will supply – for a fee – a man with a gun. The fee depends on how difficult it is to get to the target and, of course, on how much you can afford to pay.

In the course of this job I do my best not to judge people. Whoever they are, wherever they're from, it's my role to listen, to understand and to develop a rapport. I like to think I managed it with Andres the *sicario*; I even like to think I managed it in the school for Paramilitaries. But sometimes you come across an individual who is so loathsome, it's impossible not to judge them, and to judge them poorly. This was one of those – as worthless a human being as I have ever met, worse even than the fixer I'd had to deal with earlier in my stay.

He was a full-figured man – in fact he made me look positively sylph-like – and the room in which we met him was covered with religious paintings, frescoes and crucifixes.

I guess he must have thought he had a lot to ask forgiveness for. He said he spoke for the Paramilitaries. Whether that was true or not, it was difficult to say, but what he told us certainly had the uncompromising ring of truth. The impression I got was that he was being employed by them to put their point of view across – this was the kind of guy who would do pretty much anything if the price was right – or maybe he just thrived on dangerous situations, or creating an atmosphere of fear.

I asked him what it was that he and his kind did in Medellin. 'We don't agree with the injustice taking place in this country or this city,' he told me. 'Many times the legal system here catches a rapist or thief and then they get released onto the streets and continue to offend. These are the people we either try to kick out or bring to justice. We impose our power. We like law and order. We don't like lowlifes.'

I thought of Judith Vergara and wondered whether he thought she was a lowlife. I asked our man if he knew who was responsible for her death.

'Everyone knows she was murdered by illegal Paramilitary groups. Look at this girl – the way she was fighting along-side the Mothers of Candelaria. Look at how worthless her life was.'

Judith Vergara had four children and a husband. She laid down her life for her community. It sickened me that this man felt justified in saying that her life was worthless, and it took all my restraint and a good dose of acting to keep the distaste from showing in my face.

'How much would a *sicario* have been paid to kill her?' I asked.

'In your money,' he replied, 'it could have cost £125. Or even less. Fifty or a hundred pounds.'

Fifty pounds for a mother's life. As he told me this, his voice was a monotone, uninterested. He almost sounded bored – as though he were doing nothing more stimulating than ordering a pizza. Judith Vergara's life and death meant nothing to him; he was only interested in how much money he could make out of such a transaction. And his excuse – that because the police and the judiciary weren't good enough at doing their job, it was down to people like him and those he worked for to clean the streets of scum that's on them – well, it didn't cut it with me. Supplying young kids with guns to go out and kill other young kids is not my idea of cleaning the streets.

Despite my loathing for the man I was talking to, or perhaps because of it, I had the impression that he wasn't long for this world. He associated with the *sicarios* and the Paramilitaries not out of a sense of shared ideology, but for the money. It's a dangerous game, and he was scared. Scared to walk the streets. Scared to talk to us. Scared to be recognized. Nevertheless, he was the first person on the Paramilitaries' side of the fence who was prepared to admit openly that demilitarization was a sham. The Paramilitaries were still cleansing the streets; and they were still recruiting.

I might have despised everything this guy stood for, but when he agreed to try and put us in touch with one of his bosses, I knew that I would have to put up with his acquaintance for a little while longer. It wasn't a prospect that filled me with much glee.

We were a little closer now to our goal of speaking to a Paramilitary leader, but it was going to take time for the assassins' agent to set things up. In the meantime, I had one more line of enquiry I wanted to follow. Jorge Ceballos had told us that the Paramilitaries were recruiting from the ragtag street gangs in the slums around Colombia's main cities. I wanted to find out for myself if this was true. I wanted to speak to the gangs themselves and find out what was happening on the ground. No one in the street gangs around Medellin was willing to talk to me, however. And so I had to travel out of the city, nearly 300 miles to the north, to the tourist destination of Cartagena.

Cartagena is s a beautiful city on the Caribbean coast, very Hispanic in flavour but with a touch of the West Indies and impressive defensive walls. But like so many beautiful places in Colombia it has a darker side. Outside the city's magnificent ramparts are the slums – the *barrios* – home to around eighty different street gangs. One of them had agreed to talk to me. All I had to find them with was an address and a name: Diablito.

Diablito's neighbourhood is not the one the tourists see. Not by a mile. After the favelas of Rio and the slums of Medellin, I thought I was used to the kind of sights I would see in the Cartagena *barrios*. But it was while I was in Diablito's neck of the woods that I came across a sight I genuinely hope I never have to revisit.

Most of the houses in the *barrios* I had seen were built on a slope. This has one major advantage: sanitation. The slum houses clearly have no toilets, so the occupants shit into pipes that lead out into the street, or into a little container which is then emptied on to the street. When it rains, the water washes away the accumulated human excrement. As I wandered around Diablito's neighbourhood, however, I suddenly became aware of a terrible smell. We had come to a point on the hill where it levelled off slightly before continuing in a steep gradient, and as I turned a corner, it became clear what the smell was. When it rains, all the human shit is washed down the hill and accumulates on this little plateau. The weather was hot, and it was festering. I stopped in my tracks, and as I looked ahead the ground seemed to be moving. It was a minute before I realized why. The sea of human excrement was covered with flies. They were having a good old feast. Suddenly they flew up – a thick black cloud of them that made me fight to hold on to my breakfast. It really was all I could do to stop myself from gagging, and I couldn't believe that there were houses on this part of the street. But there were. People seem to be able to get used to anything, after a while.

Diablito's gang had a dangerous reputation. Rumour was that they'd been involved in a number of killings and so, although I knew that they were young, I also knew that I had to tread carefully in their presence, so it was with trepidation that I approached the door to their compound. It was covered by a black metal grille, and when I knocked on the door, Diablito himself, the gang leader, answered. His eyes were covered by the peak of a red baseball cap, and he shook my hand warily through the grille before letting me in. The compound was a poor place, but he showed me round with pride. Threadbare clothes hung on washing lines all along the dilapidated walls of the tiny buildings; girls who looked barely old enough to be at school held babies to their breasts. But despite the poverty there was an air of relaxed pride about the place. Everyone here, it seemed, was pleased to be in Diablito's gang. The youngest of them, I was told, was ten years old.

Diablito introduced me to his friend Elkin. He also wore a baseball cap – a white one – and he cradled a shotgun nonchalantly as we spoke. And between them they painted a startling picture of what life was really like on the streets of Cartagena. Elkin and Diablito had been part of a gang ever since they were small children. There was always someone trying to beat them up and mug them, and as a gang they were able to stand up for themselves. Now, if anyone has a problem with Diablito's gang, they know where to find them.

I wondered how often these young men found themselves fighting. 'Every time it rains,' Diablito replied.

This surprised me. In my experience, most gangs avoided bad weather like the plague – a simple human urge to avoid getting wet. But I couldn't argue with Elkin's explanation. 'When it rains,' he said, 'the police don't turn up. They don't come out because they get wet, and they look disgusting and stink.' He laughed as he told me this, and it was pretty obvious what his opinion of the police was.

What I really wanted to know about, however, was the Paramilitaries. To what extent had they penetrated the *barrios*? Was it true that they were trying to recruit from the street gangs, to take control of them? Elkin and Diablito didn't mince their words. 'The Paramilitaries are very active in this area. Because they are well armed and have support from the police . . . They have a lot of guns. They want to take over the city. To kill.'

So much for decommissioning.

Elkin told me a shocking story. 'They killed a friend of mine,' he said. 'He was walking down the street, holding his son by the hand. And he asked the Paramilitaries, "Why are you looking for me when I have done nothing to you?" And when he turned round, they shot him in the head. And he fell on the floor still holding his child. They killed him like a dog in the street.'

Diablito confirmed this story. 'For them, the more they kill the better.'

I was under no illusion that Diablito and his gang were angels. They were desperately poor, and what little money they came across was not earned by honest means. Their main source of income came from stealing jewellery and handbags from tourists in the old town at night. I'd never justify the way they made a living, but after spending time with them I could see that it was actually all part of a struggle for survival. After our first meeting, we took a couple of the gang to a restaurant and they thought all their Christmases had come at once. They have very little and like many in this world they have to compete for food – all the while living with a backdrop of tourist hotels where wine costs fifty dollars a bottle.

The Paramilitaries argue that they want people like this off the street: they're bad for the tourist trade, they commit crimes and they don't look nice. And it's true – I don't want my bag stolen or to be robbed at gunpoint. But I couldn't help but be a little cynical of the Paramilitaries' claims that they are cleansing the streets for purely altruistic reasons. Off camera, I spoke to the mother of one of the gang. 'I'm worried for my son,' she told me. 'The Paramilitaries come round and they collect for people to be cleaned off the street, and one of the people they're trying to clean away is my son. They know who I am, but I still have to pay them money. I feel like I'm paying just to keep him alive.'

It's simple extortion. These people have almost nothing, but they're paying protection money to a supposedly demob-ilized force to supposedly keep crime off the streets – and yet the very people they are paying think nothing of shooting a man dead in front of his child.

Street gangs like Diablito's have a simple, stark choice. Either they start working for the Paramilitary group or they die. Astonishingly, Diablito's gang has so far refused to be recruited. I asked them what they would do when the time comes – as it inevitably will – for the Paramilitaries to come after them.

'We're going to keep a low profile,' Elkin told me, 'so they leave us alone.'

But weren't they scared of them?

'Truth is, I have never been scared of them because if they don't bother me, I don't bother them. But if one day they cross my path, well, I will have to fight them. I don't let anyone mess with me.'

It's an audacious claim. I know that if I were in their shoes, I'd be a little less bold.

It was a couple of days later that the call came through. Our loathsome *sicario* agent had had a breakthrough. A meeting had been arranged with a Paramilitary leader. At last I was going to be able to get together with one of the shadowy figures who'd had so much influence over all the people I had met since I arrived in Colombia. This was a man who could have ordered the deaths of at least a couple of hundred people. I can't say I wasn't a bit apprehensive.

The Paramilitary boss was based about two and a half hours' drive outside Cartagena. The meet was to take place at night, and as a safety measure we arranged for the British authorities to be informed if we weren't back by two in the morning. If that happened, it meant something had gone wrong. And as I had learned during my stay, when something goes wrong in Colombia, it goes very wrong. Whether the authorities would have done anything to help us is another matter; most likely they'd have thought it was our own damn stupid fault to go after such people in the first place. Most likely they'd have been right.

Marta had her characteristic effect on the *sicario* agent, who insisted that she travel with him. I was to follow in another car, a white Nissan Jeep. Things started badly when the agent zoomed off like he was driving a Formula 1 car. I floored it in pursuit, cursing him. We were supposed to be travelling discreetly – this wasn't the sort of journey where we wanted to be stopped and asked inconvenient questions – but that was proving impossible as we sped down roads designed for much slower-moving traffic.

Suddenly he stopped. I followed suit. He climbed out of the car and pointed at the Nissan. 'You've only got one light on,' he said. 'You're drawing attention to us.'

I bit my tongue.

It was on the road to Cartagena, though, that my ineptitude as a secret agent came to the fore. Arriving at a roadblock with a tollbooth, we slowed down and I watched the *sicario* agent hand over a few notes. The barrier rose and he drove through. For some reason and not having any money, I assumed that he would have paid for us, so I carried on past the tollbooth, giving the woman a friendly wave as I did so.

Bad move. She slammed the barrier down on the top of the white Nissan, bending the barrier itself and not exactly leaving the car in peak condition. Suddenly we were surrounded by police taking more than a vague interest in us. I apologized profusely, turning on whatever charm I could muster. When they saw the camera equipment in the van, I told them we were here to film a documentary on the fascinating wildlife of the region. I won't reveal which TV company we claimed to be from – suffice to say that it wasn't Sky. In the end the police seemed to believe us and, astonishingly, we were allowed to drive on.

It was eerily dark now that we were away from the bright lights of the city, a little stressed by the journey and by the fact that we were heading into an extremely dangerous situation. The man we were going to meet was a field commander with more than 400 Paramilitary soldiers under his command. I could only guess at how many killings he had ordered. This was a wanted man. The families of his victims wanted him. The authorities wanted him. We knew pretty much what would happen if those two groups of people caught up with him while we were with him. At the time I remember thinking that this was the most dangerous thing I'd ever done. That was no exaggeration: going to meet this guy was foolhardy to say the least.

We finally arrived at the rendezvous point. As I got out of the car it was damp and dewy. There was a smell of horses and cows, and I could hear the sound of animals all around. Men surrounded us, all of them as jumpy as hell, clearly half-expecting this to be a set-up, for us to be police, or at least in league with them.

We were completely isolated, miles away from civilization or anyone who could help us if things went pear-shaped. The house itself was not the commander's but clearly belonged to someone who had Paramilitary sympathies. A lot of care had gone into making sure that there was nothing in the place to identify the owners: photographs had been turned face down; any pieces of crockery and furniture that might be memorable had been removed. Once again, the good old Colombian paranoia, but then I suppose these people had more reason to be paranoid than most.

The time finally came for me to meet the Paramilitary commander. He was a tall man, and a lot thinner than I was expecting. Less of a fighter. Looking back I guess it made sense – this was the man who handed out the orders, the man who told people to go out and shoot to kill. He wasn't the one who pulled the trigger.

Throughout my time in Colombia I had been searching for a member of the Paramilitaries who would openly admit to not having demobilized. Finally I had found one, and he was utterly unrepentant. 'I never wanted to demobilize,' he told me, 'because I never had much faith in the politicians who are currently in power. And we don't want our children to grow up with this same war and political manipulation which makes us look like criminals in the eyes of the world, like a race that must be exterminated.'

As he spoke, he sounded completely convinced by his own argument. He sounded angry with his own government and convinced that the Paramilitaries were the only solution to Colombia's problems. I wondered how he could be so sure.

'In most of the violent neighbourhoods we run urban militias. We have people who help us clean up the area in conjunction with the police.'

But what exactly did he mean by 'clean up'?

'When we talk about social cleansing,' he explained, 'it means combating all the crime in the community. There are people who are trying to make money even if it means stealing from others. So for us to control this, we have to eradicate these individuals. To get rid of this stain on our people.'

I thought of Judith Vergara again, laid out barefoot in her coffin, her family wailing beside her. I wondered if he thought she was a stain on his people, but I sensed it would not be a good question to ask.

'While there are guerrillas in Colombia,' the commander continued, 'there will be destruction. There have to be Paramilitary groups because we have to fight them, and we can't allow our country to destroy itself. We can't give any control to people who are bloodthirsty.'

I thought of Diablito and Elkin. Of their friend who was shot in the street in front of his own child. If the people who had committed that act were not bloodthirsty, I wondered who was.

We had heard about social cleansing, but this was the first time I had met anyone who actually carried it out. I was struck by the conviction with which this man spoke. He believed in what he was saying. He believed in his heart that what he was doing was essential to combat the crime on the streets of Colombia. As I took my leave of him, I couldn't help but consider this strange contradiction. I had no doubt, from what I had seen and learned, that the Paramilitaries presided over a reign of terror on Colombia's streets; I knew that their *sicario* gangs instilled terror in ordinary citizens; and I knew beyond question that in many cases the Paramilitaries were the cause of, not the solution to, a lot of Colombia's troubles. And yet, clearly, some of those involved genuinely believed in what they were doing. They genuinely believed that their actions were right. And there was nothing on earth that was going to make them throw down their guns.

As we left, it was becoming more and more clear to me that if I had come to Colombia looking for easy answers to their complicated situation, I was going to leave disappointed. Our journey back seemed to highlight that fact. I don't know how far outside Cartagena we were when the car ahead suddenly braked. Everyone inside the Nissan was jolted violently as I in turn put my foot on the brake.

'What's the matter?' I murmured. Then, peering through the windscreen, I saw something on the road, lit up by the glare of the headlamps from the car in front.

Not big. About the size of a man.

I watched in horror as a body was lifted from the road by the *sicario* agent and his assistant.

How it had got there was anybody's guess. Drunk, maybe. Or high. Or maybe there was some more sinister explanation. Whatever the truth, locals appeared from nowhere and started to blame us for the man's death, saying we'd

37

knocked him down. To say it was tense would be an under-statement – we got out of there as quickly as we could.

Dead bodies in the road in the middle of the night. Somehow it seemed to sum up much of what I'd seen and heard in Colombia.

It would be easy to be disheartened by Colombia: to witness the violence, to speak to the many people affected by it, and to come away with nothing but a sense of despair. But strangely that was not how I felt when my time there came to an end.

Certainly, I had seen the darker side of human existence there. I had met assassins and thugs, witnessed poverty on a large scale and come eye to eye with ordinary individuals who had suffered more than I could begin to comprehend. Sometimes I still think about Andres the *sicario* wandering half-stoned through the streets of Medellin in his Angel shirt. I wonder if he managed to keep his half-hearted promise to God and permanently kick his habit of killing or had he himself become a victim.

The sorry truth is that the odds stacked against him. In a country where there are numbers of people prepared to order killings, there will always be work for the *sicario* gangs. And in a place where poverty and affluence live hand in hand, there will always be crime on the streets. If it truly is the Paramilitaries' goal to cleanse Colombia of the per-petrators of such crime – kids like Diablito and Elkin – then they have their work cut out.

It would be easy to be overwhelmed by the hopelessness of it all, but somehow I wasn't. Because as well as all the dreadful things I had seen, I had seen reasons for optimism too. I had met the Mothers of Candelaria, and learned about Judith Vergara's selfless bravery; I had encountered the warmth of the Colombian people, and met some people like

Jorge Ceballos who refused to be deterred by the violence of the Paramilitaries and the guerrillas, who insist that their country is worth saving, that it *can* be saved.

The total demilitarization of the Paramilitaries was not a fact: that much I did know. But many of them have thrown down their arms and I think that alone has given the Colombian people some sort of hope. Those ex-Paramilitaries I met in the school may have known that the process is far from being complete, but they were at least being educated and given skills. They were being given a way out. Whether they will take it remains to be seen, but they have an option. And although life in Colombia is hard, it is not as bad as it was a decade ago. Even a half-hearted demilitarization is better than none at all, and with good people like Jorge Ceballos on the scene there will always be hope for this troubled country. I truly believe there will eventually be peace there. And when I return, which I would like to do some day, I hope more than anything that progress will have been made.

2. Poland

By anyone's standards, Poland has had a rough seventy years.

Of all the countries involved in the Second World War, it was Poland that lost the highest proportion of its citizens. Over six million people – approximately half of them Polish Jews – died. Most of the Nazi death camps, including Auschwitz, were situated there. At the end of the war its borders were moved west, causing the forced migration of millions of people, and the Soviet Union installed a communist government that was not overthrown for another forty-five years. They've been overrun from the west and from the east; they've been brutalized, suppressed and displaced, so perhaps it's not surprising that they're a fiercely proud race, or that almost everywhere you go in their country you see the slogan *Polska dla Polaków* – 'Poland for the Poles' – graffitied on walls.

In a country so badly served by the Nazis, it might seem surprising to see people throwing Nazi salutes and shouting '*Sieg Heil*'; it might seem surprising to see the swastika flag being waved; it might seem surprising to see Adolf Hitler referred to in terms of reverence. But that's exactly what I found when I travelled to Poland in an attempt to infiltrate what I had heard were the hardest, toughest, most violent football gangs in the world.

There was once a time when no one could touch English football hooligans for violence. The ICF and the Salford Reds were the firms to beat and even today, long after the glory days of their reign of terror, their reputation echoes throughout European football. The Polish gangs, though, seem to want to go one better. They want to be harder. Tougher. More violent.

People die at football matches in Poland. It's just the way things are.

I had travelled to Kraków in my quest to come face to face with some of these guys. It's a beautiful city – a world heritage site that tourists flock to. Hitler decided that it would be his base in eastern Europe; Stalin specifically instructed that it should never be destroyed. And when I first arrived there I had the sense of a place that was striving to be somewhere else – Madrid, maybe, or Vienna. It was a cosmopolitan city, and yet the people I was here to see, and the places I would end up going, would show me a very different side to the country than the one most tourists end up seeing.

I had come to meet football hooligans, so where better to start than at a football match?

It was a regular Saturday afternoon, and one of the local Kraków sides – Wisla Kraków – was entertaining a team from out of town – Lech Poznań. Like a lot of the 'fans', I wasn't going to watch the football; I was going to see it kick off in a very different way. I also wasn't going to go straight to the game. At the invitation of the Kraków police, I first headed to the train station accompanied by an elite squad of heavily armed riot officers. They had given me permission to join them as they greeted an arriving trainload of Lech Poznań supporters.

Poznań is a city in west-central Poland, and its team is named after Lech, Poland's legendary founder. I never made it there, but by all accounts Poznań is an impressive place,

41

one of the oldest towns in Poland and an important historical and cultural centre. From the way the riot police were
tooling up, however, I could tell that the visitors they were
about to welcome to Kraków weren't going to be poets and
artists, and they weren't coming here for the culture.

You could almost taste the anticipation as the riot police
strapped on their thick black body armour. They had riot
shields and sturdy batons; they had heavy black canisters of
tear gas and pepper spray; they had shotguns. Their weapons
were loaded with plastic bullets that would knock you off
your feet if they hit you in the chest; catch one of them in
the face and you wouldn't be going anywhere for a while.
The police had a grim-faced determination about them: I
didn't doubt for a minute that they would use this weaponry
at the first sign of trouble. There were 300 of them congregating to meet just one train, and it looked more like they
were getting ready for an invading force than a few football
hoolies. The fact wasn't lost on me that we were thirty-five
miles from Auschwitz, a place where, seventy years ago,
other people had arrived in trains to be greeted by men in
black carrying guns. They were a very different force from
a very different country, but the echoes of that time would
inform my own trip to Poland. I just didn't know it yet.

The train station itself was on the outskirts of town. It
was a bleak, unlovely place – all concrete and electricity
pylons – made a great deal unlovelier by the fleet of black
vans that had brought the army of riot police. I arrived there
myself in one of these vans, and I was struck by how up for
it the police themselves seemed. They knew they were going
to have a fight on their hands today, and I couldn't help but
think that they were looking forward to it. Relishing it. There
was an excitement in the air, and it was contagious – if I'm
honest I would have to say that I understood their sense of

exhilaration. That I shared it. There was a weird kind of thrill to be had from the anticipation of the forthcoming encounter.

They had dogs with them too. Big dogs – aggressive German shepherds with muzzles over their mouths. Even the animals were edgy. Excitable. They knew something was about to happen.

Grim-faced and silent, the police marched on to the platform, and I joined them. The air was pregnant with the threat of violence to come.

Soon enough, the call came in on a police radio that the train had arrived at the next station along the line. The Lech Poznań boys were only five minutes away. I don't know if the dogs could hear the sound of the train on the tracks, or whether they could sense the increased tension in their handlers, but they seemed to grow even more agitated. The muzzles came off, and it was instantly clear that these were aggressive animals, trained to intimidate people. They made a bloody good job of it – one got so excited it had to be dragged away by its handler. The police started putting their helmets on, tightening their boots and their body armour, checking that their guns were locked and loaded, safety catches on for the time being. They then formed up in rows – it was like watching the Roman army prepare for battle, shields raised in gladiatorial fashion.

And then, in the distance, the train trundled into view.

It had been long time coming. Poland is a big place, and Poznań is a good five-hour train ride from Kraków. A long way to travel for a punch-up, which suggested to me that the Poznań supporters were pretty serious about what they had come to do. The police obviously agreed – that's why they were so heavily tooled up – and I couldn't help thinking that if it was me arriving at that railway station, I wouldn't be getting off the train. I'd be sitting tight and going straight home.

I'd been told that the authorities had gone out of their way to make the train as uncomfortable as possible for the Lech Poznań supporters. If the plan was to tire them out and dampen their enthusiasm for a fight, I could tell as soon as they started disembarking that it hadn't worked. They were lairy and full of energy. Not all of them had their heads shaved, but most did. It seemed almost regulation. As they were searched and herded like prisoners towards the waiting buses that would take them directly to the stadium, I heard taunts and shouts coming from the crowd. There was no chanting, however, and one of the detectives told me that this was a good sign, for the moment. Chanting would mean trouble, but the welcome party of heavily armed police seemed to have put that off for a while. Or maybe they just wanted to wait a bit before they pulled the cat out of the bag. Whatever the truth, it was Police 1, Hooligans 0. How long that score line would be maintained was anyone's guess.

I noticed that a lot of the hooligans wore hooded tops and were intent on covering their faces, making sure that they couldn't be recognized. It looked like a kind of uniform, and it was explained to me that the hooligans who needed to conceal their identity had these jackets made specially. When the fans saw our film cameras, it was clear from the looks we got that our presence wasn't wanted, and all of a sudden the fact that there was a wall of heavily armed police between them and us didn't seem like such a bad thing.

With the precision of a military operation, the Lech Poznań fans were loaded on to the buses and transported to the football ground, all the while surrounded by police vans with their sirens blaring. You would think that a group

44

of high-security prisoners was being moved from Broad-moor for all the noise and commotion that was being made, but this was commonplace for match day in Kraków. Once at the stadium, they were searched again, before being taken to a special enclosure, separated from where the home supporters would be placed by wire fences covered with bundles of angry-looking barbed wire. Their tiered seating was fenced off from the pitch behind big sheets of thick iron, and surrounded by private security and police – and all this two hours before the Wisla supporters were allowed into the ground.

Match time approaches, and the chanting starts. It's clear just from the way that they're eyeballing each other across the stadium that there's no love lost between the two groups of fans. Relatively speaking, there are not many Lech Poznań supporters here, but what they lack in numbers, they more than make up for in noise. Every time the Wisla fans shout the name of their team, the Lech supporters respond with a single word: 'Whore!' As insults go in Poland, that's one of the worst.

And the game hasn't even started yet.

I notice one of the Wisla supporters on his mobile phone. He's not concentrating on the football, and he's not chanting or taunting. Quite calmly, he's looking over to the Lech Poznań stand, in the direction of another guy, also on the phone. They're talking together. These people, I realize, are the bosses, and it suddenly becomes clear to me that the violence is being orchestrated by the leaders of the two groups of hooligans. It's impossible to for me to know what they're saying. Perhaps they're cajoling each other; per-haps they're making sure it all goes off at the same time. Whatever it is, they've come for some aggro, and they're coordinating with each other to make sure they get it.

From my position in front of the Wisla stands, I notice certain symbols. The most common, worn by Lech supporters, is a white star in a circle with a line through it. The star is the Wisla emblem, but the cross through it denotes that the wearer is part of an anti-Wisla gang. It speaks volumes that these people define themselves not by what they are, but by who they hate. It doesn't exactly bode well for the rest of the match.

Within minutes of kick-off, trouble erupts. But it's not the Lech supporters that make the first move; it's the home Wisla fans who, desperate to get at their enemies, start to take on the security guards placed there for the sole purpose of keeping the two gangs separate. And from where I'm standing, one thing is perfectly clear: there's a lot of hooligans and not enough security. I might have thought that the police presence was over the top, but I'm beginning to understand just why. I watch as seats are vacated and the fans bundle up the terraces towards the security guards. Like something out of *Star Wars*, the guards wear black balaclavas under their helmets; and as the fans close in on them, they have no hesitation in coshing them with their heavy rubber truncheons or spraying the crowd with tear gas.

Instantly, like the Red Sea parting, the hooligans retreat: the tear gas is clearly doing its job. And a few moments later, I realize why, as a cloud of the spray drifts in my direction. I feel like I've walked into a bees' nest, and all I want to do is make sure that I don't come into contact with the stuff again, but it doesn't seem to have the same effect on the Wisla supporters. They just keep coming back for more, and soon the security guards are pushed up in a corner. Trapped, with hundreds of hooligans coming at them. Punching. Fighting. Unleashing a surprising level of

46

pure aggression, the fans have no weapons – they just use their fists. It seems to be a matter of pride.

Not to be outdone, the Lech Poznań fans start to make their presence felt. I hear them shouting a new chant: 'Hey, hey, Cracovia! Hey, hey, Cracovia!' It's a chant designed to infuriate the Wisla fans. Cracovia is Kraków's other football team and Wisla's bitterest enemy. What the Lech Poznań supporters are doing is the equivalent of an Aberdeen supporter going to a Glasgow Rangers match and shouting for Celtic: a neat and needling little way of winding up the opposition.

Above the almost deafening sound of the chanting, I start to hear another noise: the noise of the metal fence that separates the two sets of fans being shaken. Like a crowd of angry animals, they are trying to tear the fence down, the whole crowd moving as one. It's amazing the power a crowd of people moving in rhythm can create, like a Mexican wave of sheer force. It's perfectly clear that they could destroy that fence; it's equally clear that if that happens, it will be carnage. Police in white helmets start pouring into the ground, bravely surrounding the Lech fans in an attempt to stop a full-scale riot. The impression I have is that the Lech supporters purposely hold back at this stage. They know that if the wall goes down, the police will open fire. Their own people will be wounded or killed, and a lot of them will end up in prison. The show of force by the police pulls them back from the brink.

I found myself breathing a sigh of relief. If I'd felt excited earlier on, I felt scared now. The football stopped, but no one really seemed to care. They weren't here to see the game. They had a sport of their own, and they weren't playing by any rules. Nobody paid much attention when the Lech Poznań team coach came out to beg the supporters to calm down and let the match resume. After all, they clearly hadn't travelled halfway across Poland to be calm. Or even to watch football – many of them had their backs turned to the pitch all the time I was there.

I had known when I arrived that things were going to get rough, but I was surprised by the extent of it, by just how vicious these fans seemed. I had met up with a British journalist, Bob Graham, who specialized in Polish football hooliganism. I asked him if what we were seeing was typical. He told me that this was a perfectly ordinary Saturday afternoon game.

I wondered how these guys rated against the hooligans we used to have in the UK.

'They are hard,' Bob told me matter-of-factly. 'They hurt people, they stab people. There are a lot of people who have died in this country from the hooligans.'

Looking at the chaos around me, I could well believe it.

Bob explained that the violence we were witnessing was a social phenomenon. To understand it, he said, you had to leave Kraków and journey to some of the towns that had not fared well under the new capitalist order. To places where young people have nothing in their lives other than violence and hatred. Where the only sense of community they can rely upon is one based on animosity and hostility towards other football teams. This was nothing to do with sport, and everything to do with a sense of belonging. I'd seen gangs all over the world, and it sounded like a familiar story.

In the background, the Lech Poznań supporters continued to chant: 'Wisla needs to be fucked. Wisla is an old whore.'

Hardly a sophisticated message, but a clear one. I was keen to get out of there and find out more about why these gangs hated each other with such a murderous intensity.

*

Gorzów is a long way from Kraków, both geographically and aesthetically. Whereas Kraków is one of the most beautiful cities I've been to, Gorzów is at the other end of the scale. It's close to the German border in the far west of Poland, and prior to 1945 it was actually part of Hitler's Germany. As the Russians marched west in their push for Berlin, they flattened the city. Footage from the time shows nightmare scenes of burning buildings and piles of rubble. You'd be hard pressed to find any pre-war buildings left in this place: the Red Army quite literally razed it to the ground.

When it was rebuilt, Gorzów was no longer part of Nazi Germany; it was in communist Poland. Not renowned for their sensitive approach to town planning, the communists constructed one of their classic monstrosities. Gorzów is a sea of high-rise concrete, of functional, supposedly utilitarian edifices. Since the fall of communism there's been some attempt to beautify the facades of the buildings in the town centre, but no amount of beautification can hide what the city really is. And if they've made an effort with the town centre, the suburbs of Gorzów are a monument to neglect.

It's known as Poland's forgotten city, and this was where we were headed.

It had been a long journey, by train across the bleak flatness of the Polish countryside, and then by car – a white-knuckle ride of a couple of hundred miles that we seemed to cover in about an hour, thanks to a driver whose right foot had an enthusiastic relationship with his accelerator pedal. We had heard that Stilon Gorzów, the city's football team, had a fearsome gang of hoolies to its name. They called themselves the Stilon Fighters, and though the team itself was only third division, the firm that followed it was positively Premiership. They had a reputation all over

Poland as one of the hardest gangs of football hooligans in the country, and we'd made contact with a guy who had an in with them.

His name was Tomek. He wasn't a Stilon Fighter himself, but he was a local lad and he knew the right people. We met Tomek on his own turf, at a place dwarfed by graffiti-stained concrete apartment blocks. He was a big man. Tough. Strong. He had a serious, angular kind of face with a fighter's flattened nose, and you could tell just by looking at him that he wasn't a man to mess with. At least, that's what you'd have thought.

Other people, however, clearly thought differently. Tomek's face was cut and bruised. Just one look at him was enough to tell me he had taken some serious punishment, and recently. I asked him what had happened to his face. He was pretty matter-of-fact about it.

'I said hello to these guys who always hang around in the alley,' he told me. 'They already knew we were shooting a film here, and that's when it kicked off.'

In other words, the local Stilon Fighters had smashed the fuck out of him because he'd told them we were coming. Not exactly the kind of welcome we were hoping for. The gang thought he was a grass, and on the wall of the apartment block where Tomek lived with his mum (it's amazing how often people like this live with their mum!) they had graffitied words to that effect. I couldn't help thinking that it was a brave man who walked freely around an area like this after being labelled a grass by a gang with a reputation like that of the Stilon Fighters. I guess he didn't have much choice.

The estate was practically empty. It later became clear that the Stilon Fighters knew we were coming and had told everyone to stay clear so they could deal with us. Tomek explained that the Fighters were upset because they hadn't been consulted about our arrival on their manor. Over the past three years or so their reputation for brutal violence had been on the increase, and now they felt that they were above the law. That they owned the place. It seemed they were reluctant to speak to us, and I thought that this might cause a problem for our film. I needn't have worried, however. We weren't going to have to hunt them out. In fact, quite the opposite. The Stilon Fighters soon tracked us down as we wandered the streets with the man they thought was a grass.

They were intimidating as they approached us, five or six of them with an aggressive swagger. These people were young, in their early twenties – disaffected youth searching for an identity. You didn't have to be a social theorist to work out why they were so aggressive; you just had to look around you. Stack people up together, confine them in little concrete boxes, and chances are they're not going to behave well. You might as well lock them up in prison. Individually, aside from the fact that they were all pumped up on steroids, there wasn't a great deal to separate this lot from any number of ASBO-seeking kids on your average British council estate. But these people don't work individually. They hunt in packs, and it's in packs that they're at their most dangerous.

As I chatted edgily to Tomek, a group of three or four Stilon Fighters surrounded us. Like the hooligans I'd seen at the Wisla–Lech Poznań game, they wore hooded tops as a kind of uniform. One of them barked at Tomek not to answer my questions; Tomek, in turn, appealed to them reasonably not to start, not to let things escalate. These guys weren't here to listen to reason, however. They pushed the cameraman and made it perfectly clear that if he didn't turn the camera off there would be trouble. Or, as they put it: 'Stop filming or you will get fucked.'

You never know how you're going to react in situations like this. Sometimes you become paralysed with fear; other times you do your best to defuse the situation. On this occasion I just felt pissed off. There was something about this lot that irritated me: the way they kept spitting at the camera, their ill-deserved swagger. At the same time we all knew how this could end. We knew that this lot would just gee each other on and that the situation would get worse. As if to underline this fact, seemingly from nowhere, more of them appeared, and suddenly we were surrounded by fourteen or fifteen of them. Things could easily have turned very nasty. Each of them would want to be seen to be braver than the others, and we'd end up being the punchbags. Andy, the cameraman, was attacked twice. Bravely, he carried on filming, but eventually he switched the camera off and we got out of there. We'd been left in absolutely no doubt that we weren't wanted in that particular neighbourhood. If we were going to speak to the Stilon Fighters, we were going to have to find another way in.

The Stilon Fighters might not have wanted anything to do with us, but our research had told us that Gorzów was also home to a pretty unsavoury bunch of neo-Nazis affiliated to the football hooligan gangs. I had an appointment to meet two of them.

They lived on the other side of town to Tomek. The architecture was different here. More ghetto-like. You could almost see the people being rounded up for the camps seventy years previously. It was a particularly poor place. Desolation seemed to seep from the very walls of the buildings. Gorzów was once home to the state-owned Stilon

Every week, the Mothers of Candelaria hold a vigil for family members or friends believed to have been kidnapped by FARC guerrillas and Paramilitaries

Street kids playing up to the camera in Medellin

Inside the classroom of a training school for former Paramilitaries pardoned by the government on the condition they put down their weapons and start a new life

The police get ready to welcome Lech Poznań supporters off the train

I walk into a cloud of tear gas at the Lech Poznań–Wisla game

The Cracovia–Wisla game: the police move into the Cracovia stands

Fans set fire to the flags of their enemy's team

Things kick off at a football match in Gorzów

The Stilon Fighters leave their mark in Gorzów

A neo-Nazi I met in Poland

Hanging out with the twins, Python 1 and Python 2

The 7/7 gang is one of the biggest and most dangerous gangs in East Timor

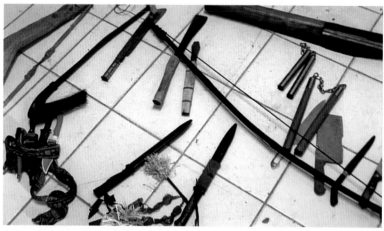

A small collection of weapons confiscated from East Timorese gang members in recent months

The largest gang on the island, PSHT, takes great pride in its martial arts skills

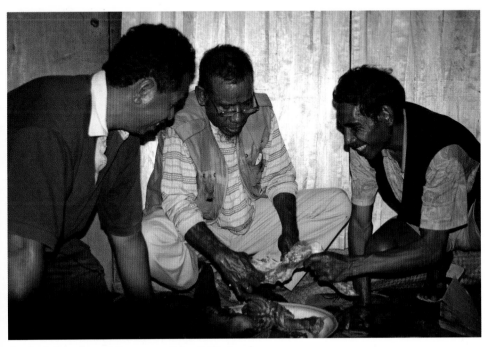

A pig is butchered for one of the 7/7 rituals

Buildings on fire in Dili after the new prime minister is announced

With President José Ramos-Horta, who was the subject of an assassination attempt two years after this picture was taken

chemical plant – hence the name of the football team – which used to provide most of the employment in the city. Since the collapse of communism, however, the economy of Gorzów has been in a desperate state, with unemployment running at 20 per cent. No wonder, then, that I was not finding myself in affluent suburbs.

In Poland it seemed to me that people reacted to economic hardship in different ways. Some hankered after the old days, the days of communism when everyone had a job and a flat and there was no crime on the streets. Others had gone in a different direction, as a result of which extreme right-wing groups had been on the up across the country. As I walked into the bowels of one of the concrete towers, I saw indisputable evidence of this. Standing out from the rest of the omnipresent graffiti was an unmistakable shape. A Celtic cross with a circle around it: the white power symbol. The people who lived in this place had marked their territory. This wasn't somewhere you wanted to be unless your skin was the right colour.

The guys I was meeting were twins, and they rejoiced in the names of Python 1 and Python 2. Their heads were shaved and they were well built and stocky – they must have looked at me and thought that I was their long-lost cousin. I was greeted slightly warily at the bottom of the stairs of their building by Python 1. His forehead was covered with cuts. Unless he had a particularly bad problem with facial hair, I didn't think they were caused by shaving. He was abrupt and slightly distant as he led me to the room where our interview was to take place. Inside the apartment block it was grey and run-down, with that same smell that seems to follow impoverishment all around the world. Swastikas were plastered on the walls. The room we entered was where they pushed weights – a lot of weights. These were the only people I had ever met who worked out and smoked ciga-rettes at the same time, which suggested to me that they weren't pumping iron for the good of their health. There was damp washing hanging from the rafters, and a general sense of dilapidation and decay.

From the off, it was clear that Pythons 1 and 2 wanted to get their point across, and they wanted to do it forcefully. I'm not sure if it was clear to them that I didn't share their views, or if they just didn't care what I thought. Clearly nobody was going to persuade them otherwise, and I rather had the sense that I was just blithely handing them the rope with which to hang themselves.

I asked them if they could explain to me what their ideology was. It was Python 1 who took up the gauntlet. 'I never liked other races,' he told me. 'They stick their noses into everything, and I hate them, so I became a skinhead.'

I noticed that I hadn't seen any black people since I arrived in Gorzów, so I wondered why it was that they disliked them.

'I just hate other races. I don't like their skin colour and them being in my town. I think that blacks should know their place.'

And what about Jewish people? Did they feel the same way about them?

'Yes, because the Jews stick their noses into everything. They want to be on top. They don't have their own country.'

It was difficult not to let my own feelings for their point of view show on my face; even if I had, however, I don't think it would have stopped them talking. Their views became even more extreme when I pointed out that Poland was famous for having been the site of a number of Nazi concentration camps.

One of their friends took over: 'There weren't enough of those places. They didn't get rid of everyone.'

I found it difficult to believe what I was hearing. 'Not enough of them were gassed?' I asked.

'They should repeat it,' Python 1 stated.

As he spoke, there was a flicker of a smile on his face. Python 1 looked like a naughty schoolboy who had just done something cheeky in class and was trying to stop smirking. At first I wondered if he was laughing at me; pretty quickly, however, it became clear that he simply found the idea of people dying in concentration camps quite funny. There wasn't much I could say to that, but I remembered the words I had seen plastered on walls wherever I had been: *Polska dla Polaków.* Poland for the Poles. For some people it was obviously no idle slogan.

We didn't set out to make the Pythons look bad. We didn't have to. They did a pretty good job of it themselves. Later, off camera, they told me that they did not believe that the Holocaust ever happened – it was made up by Jews in Europe and America to con the Aryan people. Holocaust denial is a crime in Poland just as it is in many other countries, but they seemed to take pride in their beliefs. We tried to get them to make the thirty-five-mile trip with us to Auschwitz, but they refused. Difficult to be a Holocaust denier, I suppose, when you're standing on the turf where it happened. I found it alarming that there were still people around like this.

I may have loathed everything they were telling me, but for the moment I had to put this to one side. I was there to establish the nature of their connection to the Stilon Fighters, and so I asked them if it was true that they got involved in punch-ups at football games. They happily admitted it. 'We're big in our province,' I was told, 'and generally you'll hear about us all over Poland. When we go to matches, everyone is afraid of us.'

It was a telling boast, and I started to feel like I was getting to the bottom of something. I had the sense that fighting was important to them because it gave them some kind of identity. It gave them recognition. In a world where they had precious little to be proud of, it gave them pride. I have no doubt that they would never have seen it this way, but in a country that had been destroyed from both east and west, they were fighting for their identity. What a shame they were getting it so wrong.

The Pythons were easy to dislike, but they seemed to take a shine to me, and I was invited to join them and some of their mates at a local watering hole, a place where they went to hang out with like-minded people. As we walked to the bar, we passed through a seriously dilapidated part of town. You felt closed in by the great concrete walls, and after a while you became used to the piles of rubble and debris that littered the whole area. It was like a bleak, futuristic filmset. A wasteland.

Inside the pub everyone looked like Pythons 1 and 2. They all had shaved heads, and many of them proudly wore black T-shirts with the number 88 emblazoned on them. This is a classic neo-Nazi symbol. The number 8 stands for the eighth letter in the alphabet, H, so 88 is HH – *Heil Hitler.* And whenever my new friends raised their tall glasses of beer, they shouted '*Heil Hitler*' like you and I would say 'Cheers'. This, I sensed, wasn't just for my benefit. For these people, it was everyday.

While I was there, a girl walked into the bar. She had a friend with her, an exchange student from Cuba. His dark skin, of course, was instantly noticed by the 88 Clubbers, as I started to think of them. The couple was instantly ejected, not by the management but by the clientele. Fortunately for them it didn't get any more violent than that, but if either of the unwanted punters had so much as looked like complaining about their treatment, it was perfectly obvious to me what would have happened to them. It didn't matter that one of them was female – the Pythons and their friends would have beaten them to a pulp. And they'd have enjoyed it. The threat of violence was bubbling just below the surface, and it wasn't going to take much for it to explode. Later in the evening I saw six of the Pythons' entourage pick on a guy. He was white, otherwise he wouldn't have been there; they said he was pissed, but he didn't seem much drunker than anyone else in the bar. They took him outside and beat the shit out of him. Six on one. He didn't stand a chance.

The more time I spent with these people, the more I despised everything they stood for. I despised the way they picked on easy targets like the girl and her Cuban friend, and the way they clung mindlessly to the loathsome Nazi ideology. But for some reason they didn't despise me, and the day after our night in the bar I was invited round to the Pythons' flat again. This time I was to be allowed to see the circumstances in which they lived in more detail. It was pretty illuminating.

The Python household consisted of a tiny three-room flat. This was home to five adults, one baby and a dog. It was cramped and overcrowded, but the brothers showed me round and introduced me to their family with a curious kind of pride. As we crowded into one of the tiny rooms I noticed certain objects laid out on one side, proudly displayed as though in a museum. There was a swastika and an original Nazi SS armband. Also, the Pythons showed me a teaspoon with a Nazi *Wehrmacht* engraving. These were their treasures. As we were admiring them, Python 1's phone rang.

These two were unlikely to have a jangly little Vodaphone ringtone, but I was slightly taken aback by what I heard: a voice shouting '*Sieg Heil*' at him.

'The voice of Hitler,' Python 1 told me respectfully. It was a speech from one of the Nuremberg rallies.

Nowhere in the Pythons' flat did I see anything to suggest that their passion for Nazism was accompanied by a love for football. Later, I was to meet an anti-Nazi campaigner who explained that the right wing was infiltrating football gangs because they were a fertile recruiting ground. They were full of people searching for identity or community. Full of rebels without a cause. In a country where unemployment and economic hardship was rife, many people detested the idea that foreigners were taking jobs and money that should – or could – be reserved for Poles, and right-wing ideologies were spreading like wildfire through the football terraces. It's an acknowledged social phenomenon that the right wing rises in times of economic downturn, but I was witnessing it in action. It was a frightening experience.

I spoke to the Pythons' mother. She was as proud of her boys as her boys were of their Nazi memorabilia, but to her credit she was not at all proud of the way they lived their lives. Off camera she told me that she believed this was a phase the two of them were going through, that it would pass. Well, maybe. And maybe Hitler was just going through a phase too. I wasn't sure the Pythons would be ditching their extremist views any time soon. Like any mother, she worried about her sons. She worried about them hurting people; about them not coming back after a football game or a night out. It would have been nice to be able to tell her not to worry, but that would have been foolish. She was a classic example of a Pole who hankered after the old days of communism, and from a certain perspective I could understand why. Python 2 was the only person in that little family to have a job – making pizzas part-time. They lived in a run-down area, and the difference between the haves and the have-nots must have seemed very profound to them, especially as they lived in a modern country with a modern media and could see on their television screen everything they didn't have. Back in the day, however, everyone had a job and there was no gulf between rich and poor because there *was* no rich and poor. And if her sons had been tempted to go down the path of hooliganism and gang violence, you can bet your bottom dollar that pretty soon there would have been a knock on the door and the Pythons' hobby would have been stamped on.

Next I was introduced to Python 2's wife and child. She was a good-looking woman with long blonde hair and a friendly smile. As I stood with them in the room in which they lived – a cell no bigger than ten foot by five – they told me the touching story of how they met, about how it was love at first sight. As they spoke they stood hand in hand, and they kissed almost sheepishly. 'I always dreamt about a family,' Python 2 told me, and I believed him.

I wondered if his wife got worried when Python 2 went off to football matches. She said she did. 'Sometimes I tell him to choose, the family or the match. I do not want our child to meet her father behind bars. She's one year old. After a few years of prison she wouldn't recognize him any more.' As she spoke, Python 2's face was inscrutable. I didn't have the sense that he disagreed with his wife, but more importantly I didn't get the impression that he was going to do anything about it.

Despite my dislike of the Pythons, I had no doubt that Python 2 loved his family. The question was this: was his neo-Nazi family closer to him than his biological one? Did he love football hooliganism more? There was only one way to find out, and that was to go with the Pythons to a football match. Stilon Gorzów were playing at home the following Saturday, and the Stilon Fighters would be out in force. My last opportunity to meet them had been an unqualified failure, and could easily have resulted in a collection of broken bones for me and the crew. But now that I had a relationship with the neo-Nazi gangs to which they were affiliated, perhaps I would get a second chance.

Wembley it was not.

The ground to which the Pythons took me was tiny, with little in the way of comfort or facilities. Stilon Gorzów is a small club, and there were only a couple of thousand supporters. What they lacked in numbers, however, they more than made up for in passion and aggression, and the moment they spotted the camera, that aggression was clearly directed towards us. I was glad we had the Pythons with us, as they clearly had clout. It didn't stop Andy, the cameraman, from having a couple of bruising encounters with some angry Stilon Fighters who pushed the camera away from them, and told him to stop filming.

Just as at the game between Wisla and Lech Poznań, the football was incidental here. One of the Stilon Fighters stood at the front of the crowd conducting the chants, and I heard frequent shouts of '*Sieg Heil*' and '*Heil Hitler*'. The opposition fans arrived just before half-time – clearly the actual game was of no real interest to them either – and just as I had seen in Kraków, they were accompanied by a heavy escort of riot police with perspex shields and black helmets. As they arrived, the Stilon Fighters continued their chants: 'We will go to any fight for our beloved club.'

It was a bright sunny day, but the atmosphere was decidedly overcast. As I stood on the Stilon Gorzów terraces with Python 1 – who must have thought I was one striker short of a football team by the way I kept talking into the microphone on instructions from the director through my hidden earpiece – I was surrounded by people wearing masks or bandannas over their faces. Remembering the level of violence I had witnessed in Kraków, and bearing in mind that the Stilon Fighters had a similarly brutal reputation to the hooligans I had witnessed there, it would be an understatement to say I felt uncomfortable. Some of the gangs I had met in the past might have been more deadly than the people I was with now but few were as out of control. These guys had no agenda; they didn't want to be on the television; they didn't want to put their point across. They just liked violence, and that was what they had come for today.

During the game the Pythons persuaded one of the Stilon Fighters to talk to me. He was nervous about being recognized and insisted that we protect his identity. As he spoke to camera, he had a black bandanna over his face and a Lonsdale baseball cap over his forehead. Like the Pythons, he seemed to have a penchant for British skinhead fashion, and not for the first time I wondered how these lads would fare in a pitched battle with some of the English football hooligan firms of the 1970s and 80s. Pretty well, I'd have thought. The gang member explained in surprisingly good English – a lot better than my Polish, anyway – that everyone on the terraces that day was from the estates, from poor families with no money. Their life was on the street, and on the street strength was all-important.

I wondered what his opinion of the opposition was, and whether it bothered him that the police seemed to be fulfilling their objective of keeping the rival gangs apart. It didn't seem to worry him. The Stilon Fighter explained that their violence was not limited to football matches. They had a tradition of meeting their rivals elsewhere, away from the eyes of the riot police, and holding organized fights. I was later to see footage of one of these events, and it was a melee: thirty or forty shirtless men attempting to beat the living shit out of each other. He explained that weapons were not allowed. There was an informal agreement that all knives, guns or any other kind of armament were strictly banned. A kind of honour amongst thieves. This was bare-knuckle fighting on a massive scale.

Despite the undercurrent of aggression on both sides, there was no punch-up at the game that day. However, a few of the Stilon Fighters seemed to decide that we weren't there to turn them over after all, and so they offered to take us to one of the places they used for their prearranged fights. We were taken to a disused football field where members of opposing gangs would knock lumps out of each other. I was offered the chance to get involved in one of these events. Our director was all for me doing it, but I didn't think the great British public was quite ready for the spectacle of me getting bare-chested and lairy with a Stilon Fighter. Politely, I declined.

My time with the Pythons had been an eye-opener. Seldom have I met people who I found so difficult to like, and while I was doing what I could to feel my way towards an understanding of why they were like they were, I knew I could never come close to condoning their actions. Subsequent to this episode of *Gangs* being transmitted, Pythons 1 and 2 were given suspended jail sentences for being members of an illegal neo-Nazi gang. They claimed that we had coerced them into saying things they didn't mean, that we had presented them in an unfair light. All I can say is that we didn't plant SS armbands in their flat; we didn't replace the mobile-phone ringtone with the voice of Adolf Hitler. We didn't tell them what to say. The Python brothers' words were all their own.

The Stilon Fighters, vicious as they were, had a code. When they fought, they used their fists, like men. This code is common throughout hooligan gangs in Poland, but there are two football teams whose rivalry is so intense that any honour between their hooligan supporters is simply impossible. One of those teams I had already witnessed at first hand: Wisla Kraków. Their bitterest enemies are Kraków's other team, Cracovia.

Cracovia is the oldest existing football club in Poland. During the Second World War the German occupiers banned football along with all other sports; however, illicit matches took place, and Cracovia fans also became instrumental in protecting the Jewish community from the Nazis. This Jewish connection has endured, and modern-day Cracovia hooligans proudly refer to themselves as the Jude Gang. I could only imagine what Pythons 1 and 2 thought of that.

Wisla, on the other hand, has historical links with the police force. They are pejoratively referred to by Cracovia fans as 'dogs' – a Polish term of contempt for policeman, similar to our 'pigs' – but some of the Wisla fans have adopted this as a badge of honour, calling themselves the Furious Dogs, despite the fact that they have no love for the modern-day police whatsoever, as I witnessed when I saw their game against Lech Poznań. Anti-Cracovia chants include 'Cracovia is not a Kraków club, it is a Jewish club, and they should be beaten hard!' Cracovian fans respond with such sophisticated taunts as 'Wisla is just a policeman's bitch!'

The rivalry between the two sets of supporters went

through the roof in the early 1990s when Cracovia fans were alleged to have used knives and axes during their encounters. The Wisla gangs were left with no option but to respond in kind. As a result, among football fans in Poland Kraków is known as the 'city of the knives'. And the rivalry between Wisla and Cracovia is known to those who are part of it as the 'holy war'. The hatred between these two gangs is long-standing and intense. It's a common occurrence for Wisla supporters to be killed by the Cracovia firm, and vice versa. Unlike the Stilon Fighters and others, away from the football field they do not arrange pitched battles. Instead, hooligans hunt in packs of twelve or thirteen, searching for their enemies and going at them with knives, coshes and even guns, should they be lucky enough to have them. They even have a word for this pack hunting: *polivania*.

Kraków itself is divided into Wisla areas and Cracovia areas. The war between the two gangs is bitter, and if one of them sets foot on the other's turf, they're asking for trouble. On a tour of a Wisla part of town I saw a slogan on a wall: 'Today an enemy, yesterday a brother.' It was explained to me that this meant that if anyone leaves the Wisla fraternity, they instantly become a target. These people may think of themselves as football hooligans but their mentality seemed no different to that of any number of gangs I had encountered.

After my sojourn among the neo-Nazis of Gorzów, I had returned to Kraków. There was to be a Wisla–Cracovia match the following Saturday, and I wanted to witness for myself the level of violence, to see at first hand the gang warfare that was so famous across Poland.

And if I wanted to witness a fight, I wasn't going to be disappointed.

On my arrival back in Kraków I interviewed a woman

whose son – she claimed he was not a football hooligan – had been sitting minding his own business in a predominantly Cracovian part of town when a pack of Wisla kids had attacked him, stabbing him and beating him over the head with a metal bar. He died. This was a sobering thought as we went on a tour of the Cracovia and Wisla areas of the city. On one of the estates we filmed an enormous mural – strangely reminiscent of the wall paintings in sectarian Northern Ireland – and a crowd of people got distinctly pissed off with us. After the stories I'd heard about this lot, I took their displeasure pretty seriously.

It was interesting to compare the different parts of town, if only because there was little to choose between them. Given the harsh nature of the enmity between Cracovia and Wisla, you might expect to see some social or cultural differences between the areas from which their supporters come. In fact, there were hardly any. Both parts of the city were equally impoverished, and were it not for the graffiti and the murals, you'd have no idea whose turf you were on. The houses were no different, the clothes were no different; they ate the same food and listened to the same kind of music; they had the same economic outlook and the same drug problems; their parents were dying from the same diseases. The poverty that existed in the Wisla areas was no different to the poverty in the Cracovia areas. The kids growing up in both parts of Kraków had the same problems finding identities. And yet it would be a foolish man who tried to suggest to one group that they were, at the end of the day, no different to their enemies. Their antagonism is so ingrained and deeply felt – almost like a culture passed on from father to son – to an extent it is understandable. If your Wisla-supporting brother has been beaten up by a pack of Cracovia hooligans, it is hardly going to strengthen your resolve to put an end to the enmity. The violence is self-perpetuating: once blood has been spilled, it's going to cause more blood to be spilled. And as long as there are people around who actively want the hatred to continue, they are going to ensure that the gang warfare continues to be as violent as possible.

I knew that the forthcoming match would be a very big deal and had hooked up with John Adkins, an American of Polish stock living in Kraków. He was a football fan and a tour guide in the city. He told me that on the day of the game Kraków would be a war zone: with mounted police and water cannon, it would look like martial law had been declared. If I had thought the atmosphere was bad at the Wisla–Lech Poznań match, this would be something else. But before I saw the hooligans in action I wanted to talk to some of them, to try and understand in more detail why they felt the need to behave like this. John had an in with a small gang of Wisla supporters, but in order to meet them, we were going to have to travel to a part of the city called Nova Huta.

Nova Huta makes the other Kraków suburbs look like Park Lane. It was constructed by the communists in the aftermath of the Second World War as a monument to Stalinism. The communist regime always had a problem with Kraków. It was the artistic and cultural centre of Poland and a hotbed of anti-communist feeling, so Stalin ordered a huge steelworks to be built to create a substantial working-class – and therefore pro-communist – population in the troublesome city. Nova Huta translates as 'New Steelworks', and the surrounding estates are redolent of the austerity of communist architecture. It is grey and joyless. You certainly wouldn't choose to live there.

We were told to be in Nova Huta at three o'clock in

the afternoon, but gangs don't work nine-to-five hours: timekeeping and reliability are not at the top of their list of priorities. The Wisla firm, like most gangs, were unpredictable, and they were calling the shots. In the end they kept us waiting for several hours and made us relocate before the meeting could go ahead. No doubt they were nervous of us and our motives, and it took a lot of sweet-talking from John before they finally agreed to the meet.

When we caught up with them on a disused sports pitch in the middle of an industrial landscape there was no doubting who our guys were. They all wore balaclavas; some had heavy hooded tops and others wore hats with the Wisla colours emblazoned on them. I knew they were armed with coshes and metal bars, things that are easy to get hold of. You're perfectly within your rights to carry a hammer if you need one at work, and as I approached them I couldn't help remembering that in certain parts of the world your fists are considered a lethal weapon. I didn't much fancy finding out what these guys' weapons of choice were.

To a man, they were edgy and aggressive. No doubt they were unnerved by the earpiece I wore for simultaneous translation during our interview, and the units for the wireless microphones sticking out of my coat pocket probably didn't fill them with confidence either. As we walked over to them, we noticed that there was another crowd of hooligans watching us from the rooftop of a nearby garage. We were told in no uncertain terms not to film them, and we obeyed: given our interviewees' fondness for violence, the crew knew how potentially explosive this situation was.

We weren't quite prepared, however, for the level of hostility that they displayed. At six foot three John isn't exactly small, but these guys were big too, all of them at least six foot and looking like they took steroids like some of us eat Smarties. John and I are both big lads, but we were outnumbered by a gang of aggressive and unpredictable young men for whom violence was a hobby.

At moments like this the simultaneous translation is crucial. Get it slightly wrong, and the interview turns into a game of Chinese whispers; misunderstand someone in a tense situation, and things can quickly go from bad to worse. It's the tiny events that can trigger things. In the movie *Pulp Fiction* there's a scene where the gangsters are holding someone at gunpoint in a car. The car hits a bump in the road, and the gun goes off with fatal consequences. I knew full well that a momentary misunderstanding could be my bump in the road, and I didn't want *anything* going off. Happily, I had the benefit of an extremely good, quick and accurate translator. For all my attempt to develop a rapport with the gang, however, it quickly became clear that they disliked me intensely. My questions were stonewalled. When I asked them what they did when they went to a match, they replied, ridiculously, 'Nothing. Just watch the game. Stupid question.'

'Stupid question' turned into a kind of mantra – they kept repeating it, and it became clear that they had no interest in giving me an insight into their lives. Why they had agreed to meet us, I don't know. Perhaps they wanted to make a reputation for themselves as the hardest hooligans in Kraków; perhaps they just wanted to nick the camera. Whatever it was, I felt they wanted to give me a good slap more than anything. Only when I asked them who their biggest enemy was did I spark any interest in my questions. 'The biggest enemy is Cracovia,' I was told. 'Stinky Jews.' A sentiment the Pythons would have applauded.

Why, I wondered.

'That's how it is and always will be. That's how the elders

brought us up. It passes from generation to generation. That's how it has to be and we are supporting tradition. This tradition will never die.'

The Wisla fan's language was truly that of a fanatic. It sounded to me like he was justifying their right to violence as someone else might justify their right to worship. One of his companions took up the crusade: 'You can ask the Palestinians why they don't like the Israelis. It's a simple question. They hate each other because of faith and so on. That's why we hate each other too.'

I didn't think this would be the time to point out to my interviewees that their grasp of Middle Eastern politics was a tad simplistic – if anything was likely to bring the Wisla cavalry from the garage rooftop to the scene, it was an argumentative tone from me – but the supporter's far-from-watertight argument did bring one thing home to me. Try as they might, these hooligans simply couldn't explain convincingly why they did what they did. I had the sense that their violence simply stemmed from boredom, from a lack of anything constructive in their lives. From a need to prove themselves. They didn't know what they were fighting about; they were just fighting.

It wasn't long before the Wisla boys felt they'd said enough. 'Stop filming,' they ordered, then repeated themselves a number of times. 'Stop filming. Stop filming.' We did as were told but our equipment looked in serious danger and so did we. Time to make a sharp exit, we decided. Before the interview had come to an abrupt close, I had asked them why the situation was worse here than anywhere else in Poland. 'The most fanatical fans are here,' I was told. 'The fighters and the warriors.'

I was about to find out how true that was.

*

Match day. My third football game in Poland, and if the signs on the street were anything to go by, it was going to be my most shocking.

My habit when filming *Gangs* is always to wear a black T-shirt for continuity purposes. Somehow, for reasons that I still don't understand, the T-shirt I had on that day had a large white logo on the back with the motto 'Fast Cars and Nudie Bars'. I've no idea where it came from – certainly it wasn't the sort of thing I would ever think of buying – but as I found myself hitting the streets of Kraków with the sole intention of putting myself right in the thick of things, I couldn't help imagining the headlines if I got knocked unconscious with a brick, or worse, and ended up in hospital: 'Ross Kemp in sexist T-shirt shock'.

As it happened, getting knocked unconscious seemed increasingly likely as the day went on. Thank the Lord I was wearing matching underwear.

By now I was used to the flak-jacketed, white-helmeted police presence. Outside the ground Cracovia supporters were already congregating, seemingly unconcerned by the sight of the police with loaded shotguns. With an hour to go before kick-off, everyone was waiting for the arrival of the Wisla supporters, who were being transported as usual in buses escorted by an armed motorcade. The last time I had seen a game in Kraków, the police had managed at least to keep the violence within the confines of the stadium. It became clear pretty quickly that this would not be the case today. The Cracovia supporters were already fired up, and even before Wisla arrived there were battles in the street with the riot police. And it wasn't just Cracovia fans causing aggro: supporters from clubs that have an allegiance to Cracovia had also turned up to have a go at the Wisla fans. It was clearly going to be a riot.

In order to get the best footage, we had to follow the police; unlike the police, however, none of the film crew was wearing body armour or a helmet. As the Wisla buses arrived, the Cracovia fans went into a frenzy. They knew that once inside the stadium it would be difficult to get at the enemy, and so they launched themselves at the police, throwing anything that came to hand – bricks, chairs, bottles, glasses. The air was suddenly full of pepper spray, shards of shattered glass and other debris. I watched a sturdy iron fence being kicked in by the Cracovia fans.

On the Wisla side, the windows of the buses had been smashed out and the fans started throwing Thunderflashes – simulated grenades that make a bang loud enough to stop your heart – towards the police. Wisla wanted to get at Cracovia; Cracovia wanted to get at Wisla. The only thing that was in between the two, stopping them from getting murderous with each other, was the police. And us. We saw the fans picking up anything they could find and using it as a missile: blocks of wood, bricks, iron bars. Anything heavy that had a bit of chuckability about it.

The sensible filmmaker would have stayed well clear of the crossfire, so quite how it was that I ended up doing exactly the opposite eludes me to this day. I thought we would be relatively safe, standing behind the line of heavily armed police, but suddenly we found ourselves inundated by a storm of shrapnel. I had the unnerving sensation of being stuck between two advancing armies. From the corner of my eye I spotted something that I thought was a bird of some description; it was a paving block, and it was raining right down on me. We were forced to beat a hasty retreat. But as we did so, we caught sight of an elderly woman. In the midst of all the chaos, and despite the missiles flying through the air, she simply emerged from the back door of a restaurant, put out the rubbish, then went back inside as if nothing was going on. How many times, I wondered, had she seen mayhem like this for it to become something she could react to in such a blasé fashion?

Finally we made it safely inside the ground. As usual, the fans were segregated, but that didn't stop them trying to attack each other. Not long after the game started, burning flares were being hurled between the stands. The game had to be stopped – not for the first time in the history of Polish football – and the Cracovian manager came out on to the pitch to appeal to the fans to calm down. His plea didn't seem to have much effect so the police moved into the Cracovia stands and started pushing the fans away from the Wisla supporters to put them out of range. The flares weren't the only things burning. On both sides fans were setting fire to enemy team flags: the ultimate disrespect, guaranteed to whip both sides into a fury. Opposition scarves were also burnt. Supposedly, these had been won in battle on a previous occasion, but I couldn't help notice they were on sale just outside the ground.

Eventually it deteriorated even further into the scenes which, I now understood, were lamentably all too common at football matches in Poland. I watched as the police used tear gas and pepper spray to repel fans trying to attack them. The sound of shots filled the air, the crack of the police weapons echoing around the stadium as they fired plastic bullets into the rioting crowds. This wasn't sport. This wasn't entertainment. This was naked aggression and hatred. If those fans had got any closer to each other, people would have died.

In the past, people had died. And if something isn't done to stamp out the hooligan element in Polish football, people will continue to die.

*

I came away from Poland with the impression of having seen two sides of a coin. The hooligans I had seen and met were part of a small minority. There were plenty of bona fide football fans, families who went to matches for love of the sport and out of a genuine, non-violent affiliation to their chosen team. And the Polish people in general had been friendly, courteous and welcoming. It would be deeply unfair to tar them all with the hooligan brush.

But it was also clear that the hooligan gangs represent a massive social problem, and not only in Kraków. It is significant that at international matches Polish fans have been known to turn not on foreign supporters but on each other. So much for solidarity. So much for *Polska dla Polaków*. In 2012 the European Cup finals will be played in Poland and Ukraine. The eyes of the world will be upon this nation where football hooliganism seems to be endemic. Will they be able to control this violent minority? They'll certainly have their work cut out. The gangs I met in Poland showed no signs of wanting to do their bit to alleviate the problem. Far from it – hooliganism was a way of life for them, the only thing that gave them an identity, a purpose. It has little to do with football and everything to do with those things that gang membership so often seems to be about: the need to be part of a group, the need to belong.

The Polish police are adept at stopping violence on the terraces, but it's going underground. Come the 2012 tournament, huge quantities of advertising revenue and sponsorship will come into the country. My hope is that some of this money will find its way to the grass roots: that it will create jobs, stimulate the economy and give people a way out of the situation that leads them to knock seven bells out of each other every Saturday. The Polish people are a proud race with much to be proud about. I only hope that a bit of investment in the country will lead to the hooligan gangs becoming another footnote in Poland's troubled past.

3. East Timor

East Timor is a small place with a big problem.

Had history dealt more kindly with it, it would be an island paradise. There are sandy beaches and tall, elegant palm trees that reach up to the ever-present sunshine. The interior is a beautiful mixture of craggy mountains and lush greenery, and of course there is the tropical climate, which would make it a top tourist destination if it were not for the troubles that have racked this tiny stretch of land. But for years East Timor has been fought over, and from what I saw the fighting doesn't look like ending any time soon.

The island of Timor lies between the two major powers of south-east Asia: Indonesia and Australia. The western part of the island belongs to Indonesia, whereas East Timor was a Portuguese colony for 400 years. In 1975, however, the Portuguese left in the wake of a coup d'état in their own country. The Indonesians, keen to add East Timor to their regional empire and control the entire island, invaded. The conflict that followed lasted twenty-four years. It cost the lives of 250,000 Timorese and 10,000 Indonesians. Bloody, by anyone's standards.

The Indonesians were booted out in 1999 following a UN-sponsored referendum and East Timor became an independent sovereign state in 2002. But independence is one thing; peace is another: East Timor might have been the world's newest democracy, but that didn't bring an end to the fighting – years of violence were never going to evaporate overnight, especially as when they left the Indonesians

75

destroyed all the infrastructure they had built up. The Timorese are a tribal people who pride themselves on their warrior-like status. East Timor might have kicked out the invaders, but there was an enemy within: the war being waged between rival factions throughout the country.

A fifth of the East Timorese population are said to be gang members. Gang membership infiltrates every level of civilian life, and has even taken on religious significance, as I was to witness during a number of bizarre initiation ceremonies. There is a strong political will to rid the country of the gang problem – UN peacekeepers have been called in in an attempt to keep the gangs under control – but that end is a long way from being achieved: the gangs are too big, too strong and too proud. And, unlike other gang members I had met, in East Timor I was to encounter people who honestly believed that they had been bestowed with a magical immortality. That they would never die.

It's difficult to persuade someone who believes they will never die to stop fighting.

If I'm honest, I'd have to admit that when it was first suggested we film in East Timor, I had to get the map out to check where it was. Nestled between Indonesia, Papua New Guinea and the northern coast of Australia, it's the kind of place you could lose under a breadcrumb. Getting there is hard too – you can't exactly hop on an EasyJet flight. I had to take three planes, and one of them was a United Nations charter.

The first leg of the journey took me and the crew to Kuala Lumpur, where we waited for nine hours before catching a connecting flight to Bali. The idea of a stopover in Bali sounded good to me, but I arrived there dog-tired, looking forward to the comforts of a cold beer, a hot pizza and a warm bed. Maybe I'd be able to catch a few rays the next day as we waited for our UN transfer to East Timor.

Or maybe not.

I arrived at my hotel to be greeted by a woman whose English was about as good as my Balinese. She was all smiles and respect: I think she must have googled me and come away with the impression that I was a great deal more important than I actually am. But through the fog of our mutual misunderstanding, it gradually became clear that a special dinner had been arranged in my honour at a place miles out of town. My heart sank as I sensed my longed-for beer retreating into the distance, however, I climbed into the woman's car with her boyfriend, my cheeks aching from smiling politely.

We drove into the night, ending up at a restaurant that the owners had tried hard to make look like a hut in a paddy field. They'd achieved their aim, because it *was* in the middle of a paddy field, and it *was* little more than a shack. Fine, if that's your kind of thing, but not quite what I was after. The air was thick with mosquitoes as I was ushered in with a certain amount of ceremony. I removed my shoes as was clearly the custom, before taking my seat and scanning the menu in the hope of seeing something I recognized – alcohol of some kind, preferably, but these people were Muslims so that wasn't likely to happen. Things started to look up a little when I spotted the words 'Pina Colada'. I ordered one, and then prepared myself at least to *try* and enjoy the evening that had been prepared for me.

What hadn't been explained before, however, was that this was a bird's-nest restaurant. And we're not talking twigs and feathers, we're talking the south-east Asian speciality made from the hardened spit of the much-prized cave swift. Everything on the menu was made from the stuff. My pina colada consisted of coconut milk to which some of this precious substance had been added. Once it comes into contact with liquid, it softens and becomes gloopy and gelatinous. The end result was rather more like drinking an enormous worm than I would have ideally liked, but as I knew bird's nest was expensive, sought-after stuff, I did the honourable thing and tried to keep it down.

While I was enjoying my aperitif, the mosquitoes were getting stuck into their main course: me. I'm a magnet for the things, and blood was literally pouring from my ankles while my hosts encouraged everybody in the restaurant to come and sit down next to me to have their photo taken as if I was Mick Jagger. All the while I was being offered a wide range of bird's-nest goodies to go with my revolting pina colada. I thought the meal would never end, but when it finally did, my torment wasn't over. It seemed my hosts mistook me for being as rich as they thought I was famous, and with great ceremony I was shown a huge cabinet filled with delicately crafted bird's nests. Each box of the things sold for a good couple of grand, and they obviously expected me to buy one. Truth was, I could have been the richest man in the world and I wouldn't have wanted to set eyes on any more of that stuff for a long time. My hosts were less than pleased when I declined.

So it was that my stopover in the supposed paradise of Bali was not everything it might have been. The next day, however, I boarded a UN Hercules C-130 to take me to East Timor – a place where people have a lot more on their minds than the proper constituents of a pina colada.

The flight was a military aircraft, full of NGO officials and UN personnel. There were no troops, but I knew it wouldn't be long before I saw the peacekeeping forces at very close quarters. In East Timor you can't avoid them. My destination was Dili, East Timor's capital, but in reality little more than a collection of poor villages. We were told in no uncertain terms that we shouldn't venture too far from Dili: however violent it might be, it's considerably safer than the out-of-town areas. We were escorted by armoured personnel carriers as we drove to and from the airport in our Jeeps. The East Timorese, we learned, love a fire. If anyone crosses the gangs there, they were generally burnt out of house and home. The authorities didn't want us being turned into an impromptu bonfire, hence the armed escort.

Unemployment runs at 70 per cent in Dili. Unemployment means poverty. Poverty means unrest. Everywhere you look you see the UN military presence – the foreign peacekeepers a constant reminder of the violence they are there to repress. There are other reminders too. The walls are covered with graffiti. Gang graffiti. As in so many places around the world where gang warfare has taken over, the symbols of the various factions are scrawled all over the buildings. Our hotel bore the scars of the country's unrest. The reception area was protected by bulletproof glass, but it clearly wasn't sturdy enough as it bore the scars of military-sized rounds. I asked the girl at reception about it, who told me that if she hadn't been answering the phone, which was kept under the desk, she wouldn't be here. The culprits had been Indonesians, shooting up the place before they left the country. The hotel clearly hadn't had the money to repair the glass, so the holes had been covered over with cling film. Just outside the hotel there was a green space where the grass had been allowed to grow high. It was covered with the washing of the inhabitants of a neighbouring internally displaced persons' (IDP) camp. The place just seemed to ooze poverty and pain.

There are other dangers in this country, but they have

nothing to do with gangs or politics. I told our fixer early on in our stay that I had found a lovely deserted beach. He asked me where it was and I told him. 'You know why that beach is deserted?' he asked.

I shook my head.

'Sea snakes,' he said with a smile. 'Very poisonous.'

I grimaced and made a mental note not to go bathing there again. East Timor was dangerous enough without me being bitten on the backside by a venomous sea snake.

In a place as poor as this, guns are a rarity for anyone other than the military. That doesn't matter, however: I discovered on my first day that the warring gangs have come up with various intricate – but no less effective – ways of killing people. On my first day in Dili I met an Australian peace-keeper, Major Pete Conroy – a tanned, good-looking lad who did an excellent job of making me look like the ugliest man on the planet. He ushered me into a room to show me a small collection of the weapons he had confiscated from East Timorese gang members in recent months.

It looked like some kind of medieval arsenal. There were knives and spears, poisoned darts, machetes and bows and arrows. It might sound like something from the Dark Ages, but you only had to take a look on the hospital wards and in the cemeteries to see that these weapons could be just as effective as a gun, especially as the points of the weapons were sometimes dipped in snake venom. Although they were rough and handmade – the sort of things knocked up from materials anyone might have lying around – they did their job brutally efficiently. The Australians made it clear to me that if they encountered anyone carrying one of these weapons, they treated them as a lethal force; and in a country where people carry machetes to work just as someone might carry a briefcase in the UK, it meant they had their work cut out. One minute it's a tool for trimming bananas; the next it's a tool for trimming someone's skull. These were items that the Australians had either confiscated or simply found on the streets. Gathering them up, however, seemed to me to be a bit of a pointless exercise. Deadly as they were, these were rough, homemade items. The gangs wouldn't worry about losing them, because they could be knocked up again almost immediately.

Major Conroy offered to take me out with him on night patrol to an area of Dili known as Bario Pite: it was after dark that the gangs took to the streets, and if I wanted to meet some of their rank-and-file members, this would be a good opportunity.

My Australian companions were heavily armed: Steyr automatic assault rifles, camouflage gear, communications equipment – you'd think they were patrolling the streets of Basra. They had good reason: animosity towards the Aussies was running high because of rumours they had killed two people in an IDP camp. There was an uneasy silence in the part of town to which they took me, a peace that seemed as brittle as bone china but a lot less genteel. It was a particularly poor neighbourhood, and I was told that this was the most violent place in all East Timor. Looking around, I could well believe it. The dwellings were small and ramshackle – breeze-block walls and tin roofs. Pigs wandered the streets at will, and groups of people loitered on the edge of the dusty road, eyeing my armed guard with suspicion and not a small amount of hostility. As in many other remote parts of the world I had been to, many of the men wore football shirts: Manchester United, Arsenal, Chelsea and a smattering of Real Madrid. I wondered how sporting this lot would be in a fight.

I was aware that a lot of the people around me would

81

have been drinking distilled palm wine. It's one of the drinks of choice out there, as it is in many tropical parts. Palm sap is collected from trees and allowed to ferment. The distilled version is incredibly strong, and it has the tendency to make drinkers aggressive. Not what you want in a place where already violent gangs live eyeball to eyeball.

All was quiet now, but Major Conroy told me what it was like when things kicked off. 'Houses burning,' he explained flatly, 'people firing darts at each other, rock fights. You name it, and they're doing it.'

There are a large number of gangs in East Timor. Two of the biggest are known as 7/7 and PSHT, and the enmity between them is bitter. They fight for power – in this country gang membership seems to be political – and they'll kill to get it. We approached a group of lads, our intention being to find out which gang they were affiliated to. There was a tension in the air as we walked up to them, but at no point did I get the idea that these kids were scared of the soldiers. Men with guns were common enough in their world, and no doubt the Australian peacekeepers were a lot less terrifying than the Indonesian invaders that had preceded them.

With firm politeness the Australians asked them to roll up their sleeves and display their arms. If they were members of 7/7, it was explained to me, they would have distinct markings on their skin; and PSHT had their own tattoos as well. The lads quietly did as they were told. None of them had any markings on their arms. But in East Timor, even if you don't have a specific gang affiliation you still have a gang name: Zero/Zero. Anyone with Zero/Zero affiliation backs whichever gang holds the balance of power in their area at any one particular time. At least they do if they don't want to have their house burnt down . . .

*

The following day a call came in. There was a riot going on in another part of town: some UN vehicles were under attack from gang members with stones. It sounds primitive, but it's easy to underestimate how effective a stone is as a weapon. If it hits you in the head fast enough, it can do as much damage as a bullet. Unlike a firearm, you don't have to reload and it can't jam. Two hundred people throwing stones at you is a pretty serious prospect.

There was no doubt in my mind from day one that the East Timorese – even those not actively engaged in gang warfare – resented the presence of the UN forces, and it wasn't hard to see why. They were everywhere, their distinctively marked trucks visible on almost every road. They certainly do essential work, acting as a kind of military sticking plaster that stops this wounded country from exploding into violence, but equally I had the impression that the East Timorese had a certain amount of justification for their discontent. While I was there I was in a beach bar when I heard the unmistakable tones of a Romford accent somewhere behind me.

'Oi, Phil!' the voice shouted. 'What are you doing here?'

I turned to see a tanned Englishman bearing down on me. 'Actually, it's Grant,' I muttered.

'Only joking, mate!' He seemed full of the joys.

I asked him what a Romford boy was doing in East Timor. 'I've got a job,' he told me. 'With the UN.'

'Really?' He didn't look much like UN material.

'Yeah,' he replied. 'I spend three months of the year in New York, seven months here and the rest of the time back home in Essex.'

'So what do you actually do here?'

'Nothing!' he replied with a grin. 'I spend most of the time on the beach.'

I blinked. 'No, but seriously – what do you actually *do* for the people of East Timor?'

He mumbled some sort of explanation, but the truth was he didn't have a clue. He was out there living the life under the auspices of the UN. The United Nations presence is definitely a force for good in the country and the soldiers do an amazing job in difficult circumstances, but if I was East Timorese, I think I'd have a problem with what this guy was telling me. From other sources I heard the complaint that half the UN vehicles that I could see on the streets were not needed, and that the money needed to keep them on the road could be put to much better use.

When we arrived at where the riot had taken place, things were at a stand-off. UN back-up had arrived and the East Timorese had retreated. The soldiers weren't taking any chances, however: they wore heavy blue helmets with protective visors, and carried large riot shields to protect them from whatever missiles might come their way. It was pretty clear that these were people who were constantly expecting violence and were well prepared for it.

I wanted to get closer to 7/7 and PSHT, but I wasn't going to manage that surrounded by peacekeepers. Instead, I was put in touch with a former presidential bodyguard and youth worker called José Santos, who was half Timorese, half Australian. He had a spot of malaria when we hooked up, but it didn't seem to worry him that much. When the government held talks with the gangs to try and quell the violence, José was involved, and now he runs a hostel where former gang members can try and rehabilitate themselves. He's a good man, and he's fighting a difficult war. But José used to be in the Australian SAS, so he knows a thing or two about fighting, and as he drove me into the slums of Dili, he explained the East Timorese mindset to me in more detail.

'The East Timorese are very proud of the fact that they come from a warrior culture,' he explained. 'If you look at their whole history, it's the one thing that they haven't lost. They're a fighting race, against any odds. And what's happening in the gangs is basically a corruption of all that warrior culture, of all that pride, of all that honour, of all that history.'

José's words made sense. Most of the gangs I had encountered seemed to exist to give their members some kind of identity. In a country that has been colonized and invaded and fought over, it was hardly surprising that a population that took pride in its warlike nature should turn to a violent way of expressing that identity.

I wondered how well organized 7/7 and PSHT were. José was in no doubt about that. 'They control the gambling,' he told me. 'They control a lot of the prostitution, the racketeering in the markets, the protection rackets.'

It sounded like they had widespread influence. José agreed. Estimates vary — it's not the sort of thing you tick on the census form — but he told me that PSHT consisted of about 31,000 militants, and 7/7 about 12,000. In a population of only one million, that's a pretty startling statistic. I wanted to know more, so I asked José if he could arrange a meeting with the heads of the gangs.

José smiled confidently. 'It shouldn't be a problem,' he said.

The tension was rising in East Timor while we were out there. An election had recently been held — always cause for potential unrest in volatile places — and no party had won a majority, so the population was waiting to see how power was to be shared out. The worry was that the president, a liberal, would be unwilling to appoint to his cabinet members of Fretilin, an extreme party which had done well in the elections and was affiliated with some of the gangs. You could sense, just walking down the street, the increasing apprehension. In the mornings I liked to go for a run along the beach, but as the days passed and the political instability increased, my runs became shorter and shorter. Our East Timorese fixer tried to keep me on a shorter leash, telling me not to go too far from the hotel, or if I did, to stick with him. I didn't need telling twice – I could sense the growing resentment towards me. I suppose most of the East Timorese thought I was with the UN; they became more and more reluctant to step out of my way as I ran, and looked at me with thinly veiled contempt. A storm was coming – anyone could tell that – and it was coming soon. Within days. Or even hours.

Meanwhile, José had arranged for us to visit one of the most powerful men in East Timor. His name was Fortasio de Jesus Maia de Andrade, and to look at him you would think he was a mild-mannered, almost spiritual man. But Fortasio was the acting head of PSHT, the largest gang on the island and an organization that has more members than the police, the military and the United Nations peacekeeping forces combined. No wonder the East Timorese government needed to call in the cavalry.

PSHT is a martial arts organization, and one which takes a great deal of pride in its existence and activities – which was why they were happy to talk to me, I suppose. As I set foot in its headquarters I had the curious sensation of walking on to the set of the James Bond movie *The Man with the Golden Gun*. The place was like a *dojo*, everyone clad in black martial arts outfits, and we settled down to watch a display of Pencak Silat – an umbrella term covering over 800 variations of Indonesia's most popular martial art, which the

86

Indonesian special forces had started teaching under the occupation. I had done a bit myself in the past, and was keen to see how good they were. Suffice to say that these guys were impressive, and when the offer was made to take the floor with one of them, I politely declined. My ego and my body weren't up to the humiliation I would have suffered.

Pencak Silat is a very ancient style of fighting, and its best practitioners, as well as using the body, are proficient in fighting with a wide range of weaponry, including machetes, javelins, three-pronged knives and double-edged swords. Outside the gang, people are suspicious of the fact that PSHT has adopted a martial art of Indonesian origin. Accusations are murmured that the gang has in some way aligned itself with the former invaders, but that hasn't stopped them from becoming one of the most formidable forces on the island.

The impression you get at PSHT headquarters is of a place rather at peace with itself, a community where martial arts are practised for spiritual rather than violent reasons. Everyone seems calm, and small children wander around the compound with big smiles on their faces. I suppose that when you know you have the combined force of 31,000 members behind you, you can afford at least to give the air of being relaxed. When I suggested to Fortasio that there was a gang war being waged between his organization and certain others on the island, he replied calmly, 'Our current position is that we are ready to defend ourselves. We're not going to attack other martial arts groups, but because of their provocation, we've been forced to defend ourselves.'

It was an argument I had heard from gangs all over the world: it's not us, it's them. We're just protecting ourselves. Fortasio's genteel demeanour might have persuaded me that this time it was true, but then I was forced to bear in mind that he was the acting head of PSHT; its actual leader was in prison on charges of possessing an illegal stash of automatic weapons.

I asked this softly spoken man if he had ever been injured while defending his organization. 'I've been injured more times than I can remember,' he told me. 'But the worst one was when I was hit with a poison dart. It happened when we were in a conflict with some other martial arts groups. I'd gone to the police to resolve the situation, but it was a trap and I got ambushed.' Fortasio showed me the scar from the dart, which he wore almost like a badge of honour. It was only a few inches from another scar. I asked how he got that. 'I was stabbed,' he said simply. Fair enough.

I walked around the headquarters and talked to some of the gang members. I soon lost the impression of a nice little community group. One young man caught my eye. He had twelve screws sticking out of his shattered left arm. He described how a rival gang had attacked his family. 'We were at home, having dinner,' he said, 'when some people came to attack us. So me and my mate went out to defend ourselves and our village. We ran after these guys, and followed them to their place, and shouted at them, "Why do you come at night, why don't you come and face us one on one?" Then we heard two shots and I told my friend to run, but I'd been hit. My friend tried to help me, but then he was shot in the head and died.' The kid wanted to get back into martial arts, but with damage like that to his arm, short of a miracle, it would never happen.

The general theme of the PSHT members was that they were more sinned against than sinning, but by any measure it sounded like they were involved in a gang war as violent as any I had seen. There was no denying, though, that this gang was well equipped to fight it. My next conversation was with a man who called himself Mr Lopez. He was a trainee policeman – bearing out the claim Fortasio had made that the PSHT had members within both the police force and the military – and if I'm honest, I'd have to say he came across as somewhat camp. If you met him under any other circumstances you'd be forgiven for not believing that he was a highly trained martial arts expert, a man who could kill with his bare hands. But then he told me about the time he had faced a gang of 150 people who had congregated outside his house and were threatening to kill his family. My view of him changed a bit after that.

The story he told me was dramatic, like something out of a movie. Members of 7/7 had gathered outside his house and were shouting for him to come out. He knew what they were there for – they were hardly likely to be calling round to see if he wanted to go out for a beer – but he had no choice as his family's lives were at risk. As he stepped outside, the leader of the gang attacked him with a sword, slicing into the top of his arm.

Mr Lopez fell to the ground. 'Oh my God,' he called out, 'I'm dying!'

The mob started to laugh. Clearly pleased that their victim was on the way out, their guard dropped. That was when Mr Lopez struck. Grabbing a secreted sword of his own, he made his move, slashing at his attacker.

Mr Lopez seemed pretty proud of what he had done – as he spoke he demonstrated the Bruce Lee style Pencak Silat moves he had used during the encounter – and I suppose with good reason. I wondered what had happened to the gang leader, though, and at first the PSHT man seemed rather coy.

Did he die? 'I'm believing so.'

Did anyone say what happened to him? 'I only remember I struck him once.'

Do the police know? 'They suspicion me that I'm the one that killed the guy.'

So he did die? 'That's what they say.'

He smiled as he made his almost-confession. I didn't have the impression that he had lost too much sleep over the death of his attacker.

It was an impressive story, but one that I was aware might have been exaggerated, so I asked Mr Lopez if I could see the wound on his arm. He had no hesitation in showing me. It was a vicious scar, maybe six inches long. Whoever inflicted that gash had wanted to do some serious damage. Whoever inflicted it had wanted to kill.

Mr Lopez, for all his smiles, was incredibly lucky to be alive.

From what I could tell, PSHT was a highly organized, highly efficient organization. It has members in all walks of life, from the poorest civilians to the military, some of whom have a great deal of political influence. It is widely under-stood to be closely allied to the Democrat Party and the Social Democratic Party, as opposed to another martial arts group, Korka, which is officially aligned with Fretilin. Maybe all that political influence has gone to their heads, however, because PSHT claims not to be a gang. But for an organiz-ation that isn't a gang they certainly have some pretty gang-like tendencies.

The day after I visited their headquarters José took me to the place where he ran his hostel. It was in a poor, run-down building, and it was full of poor, run-down young men. At first I thought they were there because they were trying to avoid being recruited into the gangs, but José soon put me right. He introduced me to a young man, also called José. 'José is somebody I've got a lot of respect for,' he told me. 'He used to be a member of the PSHT. He then said no, I don't want to be a member of any group. Pulled out from it. He was hunted. He's still hunted.'

Just for leaving?

'Yeah. Not allowed to.'

PSHT may claim not to be a gang, but once you're a member, you're a member for life. It sounded pretty gang-like to me.

José went on to show me a weapon used by all the gangs in East Timor. It's called a *ramba ambon*, and he'd taken two of them in the chest in his time. The *ramba ambon* is like a miniature home-made crossbow. The head of the dart has a hook in it like a harpoon, so that you can't pull it out, and the shaft is decorated with strips of rice bag to make it more aerodynamic. A good *ramba ambon* user can fire a dart every couple of seconds, and often the tips are dipped in snake or lizard poison or human shit.

I was keen to see how easy it was to make one of these weapons, and so our fixer found us somebody willing to demonstrate. As we had nowhere else to film our impromptu arms manufaturer, we set up in the confines of my hotel room. You don't need much to make a *ramba ambon* – just a handful of easily obtained hardware items, including a six-inch nail and a hammer. The nail gets flattened and fashioned into the ugly, harpoon-like dart, and the whole process takes no longer than half an hour. It's a noisy procedure, however, and not long into our session, there was a knock on my door.

I opened it slightly, standing in the gap to make sure no one could see what was going on inside the room. A member of the hotel staff was outside. 'Mr Kemp,' he asked with thinly veiled suspicion, 'can you tell me what it is that you're doing in there?'

I tried to smile innocently at him. Obviously I couldn't tell the truth – that we were fashioning a deadly weapon that's illegal to make and illegal to own – so I had to think on my feet. 'Got a problem with one of my shoes, mate,' I told him. 'Just trying to fix it.'

I don't think he believed me, but at least we were left alone for the short amount of time it took to finish. We took our newly constructed weapon to the beach for impromptu target practice. The guy who had made the *ramba ambon* was equally proficient at firing it – he easily shot the dart into the skin of a melon from several metres. It travelled all the way through the flesh and came out the other side. No one said as much, but it was pretty obvious that in terms of size and shape a melon wasn't much different to a head.

PSHT had almost welcomed me into their fold. But it wasn't just them I was interested in; I wanted to speak to their sworn enemies, 7/7, and access to them was proving a little more elusive. In order to get closer, I hooked up with the Guarda Nacional Republicana, or GNR. The GNR are military police from Portugal, the former colonial power in East Timor, and the reception they get from the locals is distinctly less frosty than that which the other peacekeeping forces receive. A lot of this is to do with communication: the GNR speak to the locals in Portuguese, one of the two official languages of East Timor, which most of them understand from colonial days, and as a result they are viewed with less suspicion. Whereas the Australians and others stay in barracks when they're off duty, the GNR can walk the streets more safely. They can go into the local bars and have a beer; they can have relationships with local women; they can work out in the gym.

That's not to say that the GNR aren't tough when they need to be. Far from it. While I was with them they showed me one of their weapons of choice, an electric taser gun. I witnessed one of their boys – a big guy, built like a brick shithouse – being tasered, and he went down like a sack of potatoes. The GNR man with the gun then approached me. 'You want to try?' he asked in a slightly creepy Portuguese accent. I declined. The GNR are well equipped with military hardwear – spending time with them is like being on a *Terminator* set – and from what I'd heard of the street wars in East Timor, they needed to be. But they also commanded respect as people: the gangs talked to them and listened to them. If I wanted to get closer to 7/7, spending time with them would be a good bet.

Unlike the Australian peacekeepers we had been with earlier in our stay, the GNR wouldn't let us travel anywhere with them unless we were all wearing thick black body armour, so it wasn't until we had strapped it on that we were allowed to go out with them one evening. Our first stop was an IDP facility near our hotel in central Dili. IDP camps, where East Timorese civilians forced out of their homes by the civil unrest end up, are depressingly numerous. As I write, the statistics speak for themselves: 100,000 people, or nearly 10 per cent of the population, live in these camps, 30,000 in Dili. There are nearly 2,000 IDPs camped out in the capital's national hospital alone, along with their livestock – goats, pigs and chickens. The government is doing its best to encourage these people to return home, offering them compensation depending on the amount of damage that has been done to their properties; but if your house has been completely destroyed, there's no way you can return. The Ministry of Social Solidarity has offered families in the camps two months rice rations if they go back home, but this is not exactly a long-term solution, and the IDP problem shows no signs of going away any time soon.

As might be expected, the IDP camps are hotbeds of criminal activity. More crucially for our purposes, they are fertile recruiting grounds for the gangs. When we arrived at the IDP camp the local police were already there, but as soon as they saw the GNR, they melted away. Much better, clearly, to let the Portuguese forces do what they're good at. As we wandered around, we saw lots of graffiti, all of it indicating that this was very much a 7/7 area. The presence of the GNR, however, with their guns, body armour, helmets and riot shields, seemed to have a calming effect on the refugees. No one seemed in the mood for fighting, but nor did they seem in the mood for talking. So, once the GNR was satisfied that all was quiet, we left for another part of town.

It was here that I witnessed how quickly things could escalate in East Timor. I was talking to a young woman, who was explaining to me, calmly and articulately, how certain gang members had started throwing rocks at her house in the middle of the night when she caught sight of some of the people she thought were responsible. Instantly she became a different person: the calm, concise young woman became a screaming harridan, yelling at the top of her voice. I couldn't understand what she was saying, but it sounded intense. As her anger became stronger, so some of the Timorese men around her started to take an interest. If it hadn't been for the presence of the GNR, I can only imagine how the situation would have escalated.

The woman's sudden change of character epitomized for

me a great deal about East Timor and its people. At face value, they are a friendly, open race; but they are quick to anger, and when that happens, the results can be explosive, violent. They go from volume one to volume ten in a matter of seconds. Similarly, the island itself is a beautiful place; but when it turns ugly, it turns very ugly indeed.

I noticed that some of the men surrounding us were wearing Aqui Jaz T-shirts – Aqui Jaz being another gang on the island – but when I asked them if they were affiliated, they shook their heads and refused to talk. Maybe the presence of the GNR was in fact making things harder; maybe the other gangs on the island were simply a lot more reticent than PSHT. Whatever the truth, it didn't look like we were going to speak to any of the 7/7 lads that night.

The following day was Sunday, the day of rest, and I set out to see two very different sides of the East Timorese character.

The people of this troubled island can be many things: warlike, tribal, hot-headed and violent. But they are also incredibly devout. East Timor is a deeply Catholic country, and despite the violence and the gang warfare an astonishing 70 per cent of the population attend church on Sunday morning. I was later to find out that many of them see no conflict between their intense faith and the viciousness of their gang activity; indeed one of the pieces of gang graffiti I read as we were driving around Dili read: 'Bible: Book You Need To Read'. Sunday afternoons, on the other hand, are rather less pious. Cockfighting is one of the most popular pastimes for East Timorese men. It has a rich history on the island and even a slightly mythical status, stories of cockfighting having entered the country's folklore. Some of the East Timorese believe that the ghosts of their ancestors are addicted to blood spilled in violence; in exchange for the death of the birds, the ancestors make the women of the island fruitful.

I had never been to a cockfight before, but there's a first time for everything, although I made my way there with a certain amount of trepidation – I wasn't there to make anyone fruitful. I'd been told that cockfighting was a big-money sport – hundreds of dollars could change hands over a single fight – and gambling, a major part of the culture in East Timor, was a means of raising revenue for the gangs. If I wanted to make contact with one of these organizations, the weekly cockfight would be a good place to do it.

Make no mistake about it, there's a reason these events are illegal in most parts of the Western world: cockfights are brutal. Razor-sharp spurs are tied to the birds' feet, and whereas in some parts of the world a referee will stop the fight if one of the birds gets even slightly injured, here there's only one destination for the beast that loses: the pot. The birds themselves are trained to be highly aggressive – a good thing, I suppose, given that it's only their aggression keeping them from a bloody and painful death. While I entirely despised what I was witnessing, however, I could completely understand how people might become addicted to it. It's an elemental sport, the result completely out of the hands of the spectators and even the birds' owners; and in a country where money is hard to come by the large quantities of notes changing hands on the pugilistic potential of a particular bird adds a certain frisson to the proceedings. The crowd works itself up into a frenzy, and when you're part of it, it's difficult for that excitement not to rub off on you. More than once during that day I had to remind myself that I disapproved of what was going on. I was there for business, not pleasure.

As I watched, I noticed that a lot of the men running the cockfights had little scars running the length of their arms: tattoos, in a way. These scars, I knew, were the ritual markings of 7/7. I had clearly come to the right place, and we started asking a few questions here and there. Sure enough, without the Australian peacekeepers or the GNR to scare people away, we met with more success. By the time the event was over I had in my hands a piece of paper. Scrawled on it were the contact details of a man who might be able to lead me to 7/7. We were getting closer.

November 12, 1991 was a turning point in East Timorese history, and like many turning points in history, it was a bloody one. This was the day of the infamous Santa Cruz massacre, a horrific event that put East Timor on the centre stage of world politics.

It was during the Indonesian occupation of the island that a delegation of foreign diplomats planned a visit to East Timor. The government of Indonesia objected to the inclusion of an Australian journalist thought to be a supporter of Fretilin, the East Timorese independence movement. As a result, the visit was cancelled. Tensions ran high, and a few days after the cancellation Indonesian troops located a group of resistance members at Motael Church in Dili. A confrontation ensued, as a result of which one East Timorese and one Indonesian were killed. The dead Timorese resistance fighter was called Sebastião Gomes, and on 12 November a memorial service was held for him at the church where he had died. Following the service a huge procession of men, women and children – several thousand people in all – made its way to Santa Cruz cemetery, where Gomes was buried. A number of marchers displayed East Timorese flags and anti-Indonesian protest banners. Slogans were chanted; Indonesian police officers and soldiers were taunted. The anti-Indonesian sentiments were clear, but on the whole it was a peaceful protest. At least at first.

What happened next is a matter of debate. Certainly an Indonesian soldier was stabbed; some say it was because he attacked a girl who was carrying an East Timorese flag. Whatever the truth, the situation soon deteriorated. When the procession entered the cemetery, the Indonesians opened fire. The protestors tried to flee, but many of them were forced deeper into the cemetery. Estimates as to the number of dead vary, but it is thought that around 400 East Timorese died that day. Two days after the massacre the commander-in-chief of the Indonesian forces was quoted as saying: 'The army cannot be underestimated. We had to shoot them. Delinquents like these agitators must be shot, and they will be.'

A British cameraman by the name of Max Stahl was at the protest and filmed the massacre. His film was smuggled out of East Timor and ended up on TV screens around the globe. It is a shocking document of a brutal day – a day that changed the attitude of the world towards the Indonesian occupation of East Timor, and paved the way to independence. November 12 is now a national holiday.

Two days after the cockfights, the contacts we had made there culminated in a meet with a man from 7/7, a gang member who called himself Mr January. The rendezvous was to happen at Santa Cruz cemetery. The symbolism of the location was obvious, but the massacre was also particularly significant in the history of 7/7 because that day a gang legend was born. A large number of gang members were present at the massacre, and many of them believe they were saved from death by virtue of their affiliation to the gang. But they don't put the fact that they remained unscathed down to strength or numbers; it's rather more mystical than that. For 7/7 have a very different way of looking at the world.

I asked Mr January to describe what had happened in his own words as we stood by the gateway to the cemetery. He pointed up at the gate. 'I was on the top there when the Indonesian army suddenly arrived. They shot me and I fell down. Then I was being trampled in the panic and was unconscious for around thirty minutes. I dreamed that an old man dressed in white, with a flowing white beard, was holding me. Then the man disappeared and I woke up.'

In another situation I might have laughed off what I was being told, but Mr January clearly believed very intensely in what he was saying, and given the East Timorese tendency to speedy, volatile changes of mood, I didn't think it would be a good idea to look too sceptical. As we walked through the cemetery, however, surrounded by many thousands of ornate graves, I did ask him if he really believed that he had been saved from death because of the spiritual nature of the 7/7 gang. 'Of course I believe; that's why I'm still alive,' he told me. 'As a human being, I believe first in God and then in the spirits of our ancestors. But I know that without 7/7 I would be dead.'

I asked him to show me his bullet wound. He was happy to do so. The scar on his back was very visible, and he told me that the bullet itself was still inside his body, shattered. He'd been lucky. I'd seen enough bullet wounds to know that this one could easily have been fatal. It was plain why Mr January thought he was invincible.

I was beginning to understand something of the enmity between 7/7 and PSHT. While the martial arts gang clearly had links with the Indonesians and their culture and history,

7/7 had played a big part in the anti-Indonesian independence movement in East Timor. But I was intrigued by the
7/7 religious philosophy, which seemed to be a curious
mixture of Christianity and tribalism. I asked Mr January if
he could put me in touch with anyone further up the hierarchy. He came up trumps, arranging a meeting with 7/7's
president, Agostino Fernandes. I was invited to one of their
secret ceremonies, an honour that few outside the gang are
ever afforded. Certainly this was the first time any TV
cameras had been allowed access to the rituals that make
members of this peculiar gang truly believe that they are
immune to death.

The compound that houses the 7/7 headquarters was a
poor place, but I suppose that was only to be expected. As
I arrived the following day, I didn't quite know what to
expect from Agostino Fernandes: I'd met gang leaders
before, but this guy was more of the order of a high priest.
In the event, the man who greeted me was just a regular,
middle-aged guy. If you saw him in the street you wouldn't
look twice, unless you had a particular interest in dentistry
– his teeth were distinctly rotten. Other than that, he seemed
absolutely ordinary. The rituals over which he presided,
however, were far from that, and before I was allowed to
witness them, I had to take a crash course in 7/7 philosophy.

Agostino met me at the entrance to the compound, shook
my hand and took me to the tiny house in which he lived
with his wife and six children. Some of the walls had been
wallpapered with empty cigarette packets – whether this was
a measure of thrift or because the man of the house was
particularly proud of his smoking habit, I couldn't tell. On
one of the walls I noticed a picture of the Portuguese
footballer Ronaldo. He had come to East Timor in the past
and been almost deified by 7/7, as a result of which he was

practically an honorary member of the gang – not that *he* knew anything about it. Taking pride of place in this meagre house was an altar. A candle burned, and there were decorative containers of eucalyptus leaves covering the table. I noticed statues of the Virgin Mary and a blood-covered crucifix. Agostino presented the altar to me with a swooping pride. 'This,' he told me, 'is part of our 7/7 culture and tradition. This is how we as members of 7/7 worship, and have done from the beginning of time.'

The beginning of time? Quite a claim, and I wondered how this sat with 7/7's Christian beliefs. Agostino had a stab at explaining further: 'When our father and mother separated, the earth was still in darkness and the things that we get from God, our powers, are a mystery, sent to us directly from God. More than this I cannot say. It is taboo. There are commandments from God. If I say any more, something could happen to me. Members of my family could be killed.'

It all sounded hazy. to me – certainly I didn't really understand what he was saying, although I was in no doubt that he believed it 100 per cent. All I managed to establish was that they have a belief system that combines Catholicism with pre-Christian animist traditions, and that they take their religion *extremely* seriously. To the point of death if any of them reveals too much to outsiders. I began to have an inkling that I was indeed honoured to be witnessing their rituals. However, it was also made clear to me that we were not entirely trusted. Agostino and his gang didn't know if we were good or bad, and so a curse was placed on our cameras. If we were not who we said we were, it was explained to us, our film would not come out. Frankly, if they came to suspect us, the camera film would be the least of our worries.

The mystical 7/7 rituals always take place after dark. As we waited for them to begin we became aware of a newcomer to the party: a small pig being carried upside down by its legs into Agostino's house and brought before the altar. It was pretty obvious that the beast was not long for this world – in fact, it would probably end up being dinner – and sure enough I watched as four or five of them held it still while one approached with a knife. The pig squealed as its throat was cut; its limbs wriggled. A plastic bucket was held under its throat to catch the blood that seeped from the wound. The pig's blood was to be an important feature of the ceremony: I watched as Agostino made the sign of the cross in the pig's blood on the chests, foreheads, ankles and feet of the gang members – a grisly kind of baptism.

As the ceremony progressed, I witnessed more of the practices of this bizarre gang. Members would sit and have seven small cuts slit into the skin of their arm or chest with a corner of a razor blade. The blade has to get in good and deep to make sure that it scars properly. Once the cuts had been made, a brown powder was rubbed into them. They believe this to be a magical substance that links their life force to that of the gang. It is this dust and this ceremony that 7/7 members believe makes them invincible – just as Mr January had said. I saw one guy who had these cuts on the top of his foot, on his knees, on his arms, on his stomach, his chest and his back.

To outsiders this ceremony may seem ridiculous. In recent years, they have faced up to the Indonesians, a vastly superior force with weapons and resources far beyond those of the gangs. In circumstances like those, a little bit of self-belief can go a long way. If you get people to believe in their abilities, if you offer them hope, you can get them to do extraordinary things. The men having their flesh sliced in front of me honestly believed that the ritual they were undergoing would make them immune to bullets. Immune to death. It's quite an advantage in a fighting force.

Not, of course, that 7/7 viewed themselves in such terms. Like the PSHT, they claimed that they were not an aggressive organization – they were just there to protect themselves. No doubt the other gangs in East Timor would say the same.

The pig that I had seen being slaughtered had given up its blood for use during the ceremony, but its input wasn't over. There was still a doubt in the collective mind of this ritual gang that we were to be trusted, and in their eyes there was only one way of determining if we were. A sharp knife was taken to the pig's abdomen, and its innards spilled all over the floor. A senior gang member examined them closely. It was the liver that interested him the most: he flipped it over, and explained that it was this organ that could tell him what to think of us. He scrutinized it. The liver was clean, he said, and therefore so were we. Lucky us!

It was a strange evening. And yet somehow it wasn't that strange to encounter this dichotomy of beliefs in East Timor. Kids on the island are brought up from an early age to believe in ghosts and spirits, alongside the more traditional Catholic beliefs that are common currency everywhere you go. That said, I'm not sure that a few cuts in my arm rubbed with some sacred mud would be quite enough to make me go and take nine rounds in the chest – or even face up to an enemy armed with a poisoned *ramba ambon*.

But if you have a gang with thousands of members who are, then there's no denying that it would be a force to be reckoned with.

*

The gang leaders I had met so far both claimed that they avoided violence; that they only fought in response to their enemies' aggression; that they were simply defending themselves. I knew that wasn't true. As if to underline what was so obvious, our fixer offered to take me to one of Dili's hospitals, to see one of the victims of the gang warfare that was so prevalent in East Timor.

I didn't know quite what to expect of the hospital in Dili. But I was quite impressed. It was hardly BUPA, and there's no denying that by Western standards it was pretty basic, but it was clean and seemed reasonably efficient. It was also full of very unwell people – there was no malingering here – and perhaps unsurprisingly the doctors didn't seem too thrilled about a camera team walking around the place. They refused to talk to us, but then I suppose they had more important things to do.

The patient we were coming to see had ended up here as a result of being beaten up in a gang attack. He said he didn't know why he had been singled out – I didn't know whether to believe him or not – but there was no denying that what he had undergone had been vicious in the extreme. A *ramba ambon* had been fired into his back; he had undergone surgery to have it removed, and the wound looked very bad indeed. His assailants had taken stones to his face, bits of which were still embedded in his skin. His jaw had been shattered; the doctors had wired it together so tightly that he was unable to open his mouth. He could communicate only through gestures, and through his wife. Our fixer explained to me that the patient had been left in the road for dead. By the look of him, he was extremely lucky not to be.

The political situation in the country was increasingly fraught, and the tension on the streets that I had noticed was continuing to rise. It's an open secret in East Timor that the gangs are heavily involved in politics, and the impending violence that we could all sense was clearly linked in some way to the political unrest. I wanted to speak to Fortasio, the PSHT leader, once more to ask him about the connection.

He denied it in emphatic terms. 'No,' he told me. 'That's not true. People like to judge us from afar. But you're here – are we training people in martial arts or politics?' As he spoke, we were watching another martial arts demonstration. His point was eloquently, if not convincingly, made. 'We are so well organized that despite the size of our operation we can control our members. We have total control and know whatever they are up to and what they are planning. Our object is to extend brotherly feelings and train people to be better human beings.'

Brotherly feelings? It looked to me more like they were training people to kill. I thought of the patient I had just seen in the hospital. He hadn't said the PSHT had beaten him up – it could have been any of the East Timorese gangs – but it clearly wasn't beyond the capabilities of this gang. My understanding was that they ran protection rackets all round Dili. A self-appointed police force there for their own gain.

I asked him about the PSHT's actual president, the man he was standing in for, who was in prison on weapons charges. He barely missed a beat. 'Although he stands accused, our president is actually the victim in all this. The real guilty parties remain free. They are the ones who are murderers, arsonists and thieves.' It's not us; it's them. The same old mantra. I didn't argue with this man who had 30,000 trained fighters under his control, but I walked away less than convinced.

I had spoken to two of the main gangs in East Timor,

and I had started to get a sense of what they were about and how they affected – and were affected by – the politics of the country. Towards the end of my stay there, however, I was offered the chance to hear about things from the other side of the fence. President José Ramos-Horta, Nobel Peace Prize winner and the most powerful man in the country, had agreed to talk to us.

We were lucky to have any time at all with the president. The tension that we had all noticed on the streets had not been imagined. The whole of East Timor was waiting for Ramos-Horta to announce the name of his new prime minister in the wake of the general election, and the delay in the announcement was causing a certain amount of civil unrest. It was obvious to everyone that the situation could escalate at any minute. Ramos-Horta came across as a conscientious, caring man. Certainly he didn't surround himself with any of the ostentatious trappings of office that he might have done: his house was simple and plain, and the overwhelming impression I had was of a man who had taken office for the genuine love of his country and not because power held any particular attraction for him.

I also came away with the impression that the president of East Timor had lost patience with the gangs – especially martial arts groups like the PSHT, Korka and 7/7. There was something upsetting about seeing this calm, peaceful man talk of his frustration in decidedly unpeaceful terms. He described the time he had called all the gang leaders together. 'I was very angry,' he told me, and by his tone of voice I could believe it. 'I said, "Your attitude has made martial arts synonymous with crime." I told them, "I'm going to leave, you will stay and talk. If you want to kill each other, help yourselves. You do it, kill yourselves here. On the other hand, if you want to engage in dialogue, talk rationally with each other, and it would be of service to your own country, well, you have a chance. I'll come back a few hours from now. Either I'll find some of you dead or you will have reached some agreement."' Ramos-Horta said that when he returned to the room, the gang leaders were talking and were prepared to sign some kind of truce. Some of them, he told me, had even stuck to their agreement.

I think it must take a special kind of person to devote their life to public service in a place like East Timor. A person of optimism. A person willing to see the good in people. Ramos-Horta told me quite categorically that he saw a way out of East Timor's considerable problems. 'If and when the government is ready to really kick-start the economy with major investments and spread the wealth in the city, particularly rebuilding housing for the poor, most of these people will gradually disappear into the mainstream.' The president clearly understood the correlation between poverty and gang membership, the correlation that I had seen everywhere on my travels. It was inspiring to talk to him – inspiring to know that there was at least one man in power who had East Timor's very best interests at heart.

Little did I know how dangerous taking such a position could be.

On 11 February 2008, some two years after I left East Timor, Ramos-Horta was the subject of an assassination attempt. A famous rebel leader who lived up in the mountains called Alfredo Reinardo ambushed him. The president was shot three times, including once in the right lung. Rushed to the Royal Darwin Hospital in Australia, he was put into an induced coma on full life support. His condition was listed as critical, and he was lucky to survive. Reinado and his men died in the ambush, as did Ramos-Horta's bodyguard. The president himself returned to East Timor two months later, his determination to bring peace to this troubled island undimmed. With a bit of luck he'll get a fair run at it, but the assassination attempt shows that this is by no means assured.

My time in East Timor was drawing to a close. But as we prepared to leave this out-of-the-way island, things were coming to a head on the streets. Barely hours after I interviewed the president, he announced his new prime minister. The losing candidate was a member of Fretilin and, Ramos-Horta believed, too extreme. Fretilin and the gangs that supported them weren't happy, and they were going to make their displeasure known.

The first we saw of it was in the IDP camp across from our hotel. The gangs were taking to the streets, causing havoc. Rocks were thrown at the peacekeeping forces – not little pebbles, but great chunks of stone that would kill you if you were unfortunate enough to get in their way. Tyres were burnt, causing thick black plumes of smoke to billow up into the clear blue sky. As we walked down the street, crowds were gathering and shouting angrily at the UN forces – and at us.

The Australian army, the New Zealand army, UN peace-keepers and the GNR poured into the streets. In a matter of hours the violence that had been forecast throughout our stay in Dili had erupted. We drove all around the capital, and everywhere we went it was the same. Deciding to follow the GNR, all tooled up with their state-of-the-art weaponry, we heard the sound of tear gas rounds being fired, and then automatic weapons. As we moved towards the gunfire, that was when I smelled the unmistakably acrid aroma of tear gas. The GNR had fired the stuff at some demonstrators, but the wind was blowing the wrong way and it was coming back to haunt them.

Tear gas is an effective weapon if you fire it locally and you're wearing a gas mask; fire it into the distance and when the wind is in the wrong direction and you've got a problem. Suddenly being behind the military strength of the GNR did not see like a great place to be as I came into contact with a cloud of the stuff. I felt as though I had been squirted with stinging-hot chilli. The gas reacts with moisture, so anywhere damp on your body – your eyes, your mouth, your armpits, even your groin and the crack of your arse – gets the sensation. And the intense heat in that part of the world ensures there's plenty of moisture on your body. When tear gas hits you, you can't speak properly, you can't breathe; it makes you want to cry and scratch, to move around and try to shake it off.

We retreated.

Despite the fact that we were at a meteorological disadvantage, the mob ebbed away as the troops advanced. But it was like cutting the head off a hydra: just as one bout of violence was extinguished, another flared up. There was a sense that everything was being organized: tactical violence, designed to stretch the resources of the police and army to breaking point. Meanwhile ordinary civilians were rushing around, trying to get home, or at least to vacate those areas where they knew things were going to get really bad. Despite being warned off by the Australian army, we kept trying to get close to the scene of the action, but it seemed to elude us. Everywhere bore the signs of unrest, however: the place was littered with bricks, sticks, arrows and burning tyres. At one point I saw an old woman hawk and spit into the street. My throat was still burning from the tear gas, so I did the same thing. In an instant the old woman was gabbling away at me. I asked our fixer to translate what she was saying.

'If you're taking the piss out of her,' he replied, 'she says she'll stab you!'

Like I say, a warrior race.

As the afternoon wore on, things started to quieten down a bit. Come about five o'clock it became clear that there had been a lull in the proceedings. All the troops we spoke to told us the same thing, though: when the sun went down, things were going to escalate. It was going to be a very long night.

They weren't wrong.

This was our last day, and while things were a bit quieter on the streets, we retreated to a place we knew just outside Dili to get some food. Relaxing with a beer and a massive steak of barbecued fish, I felt a tap on my shoulder. It was our fixer. 'Look over there,' he said.

'Why?' I asked.

'Well, just look across.'

I looked in the direction he was pointing. In the distance I could see Dili silhouetted in front of a dull orange glow. The troops hadn't been wrong: parts of the East Timorese capital looked like they were on fire. For a moment I was lost for words. I pointed at one building that seemed to be burning more furiously than the others. 'My God,' I whispered. 'What's that one?'

The fixer grinned at me.

'Your hotel!' he said.

We jumped in the car and headed directly towards the blaze. We had to negotiate our way through a series of roadblocks, and all around us buildings were on fire. It transpired that a rioter had thought about attacking our hotel with a petrol bomb but then turned his attention to the building next door. This was an administrative building where all the land records for East Timor were kept. At least it had been. Now it was a bonfire. We wanted to get some good shots of the fire, so a bit recklessly we went round the back of our hotel and approached it that way. On the hotel roof some Australian troops were doing their best to keep the fire under control, but with only buckets of water to do so, they weren't having much effect. Cheekily we started climbing their ladder up the building to grab some footage.

One of the Australians saw us. 'What the fuck are you doing?' he asked aggressively.

'Er, trying to get some shots,' we replied.

He looked at us in disbelief. 'Piss off,' he spat at us. 'We're trying to put the building out. Just piss off!'

He had a point. We pissed off.

Still on the hunt for good shots, we found some GNR troops, who we knew would be a bit more friendly. They let us through their cordon and closer to the blazing building. Being that close to such an inferno gave me the greatest respect for firefighters. The heat was unbelievable. Imagine the heat that comes off a barbecue; now imagine a barbecue the size of a four-storey house. We got as close as we could, but when we saw windows starting to smash open and gas canisters exploding inside, we decided it was time to walk away.

If it was chaos that Fretilin wanted, they'd sure as hell got it. As the evening wore on it became clear that the arson attacks were not random. Specific buildings had been targeted – mainly government and administrative buildings – in an effort to cause as much damage to the infrastructure of the country as possible. It didn't escape our notice that in East Timor a lot of the gang warfare derives from arguments over territory, over who owns what. With no records to settle these arguments, it looked like the gangs were going to have something to fight over for a good while to come.

That was our last night in East Timor. It was a memorable one for all the wrong reasons. We were leaving, it seemed to me, not a day too soon.

How do you persuade a country of warriors to put away their warrior tendencies? It's a difficult question, and one to which I, for one, do not know the answer. But I do know that something has to change fundamentally in East Timor. The Indonesian occupiers – the ancient enemy – might have gone, but they have not taken with them the island's problems. And at the root of those problems are the gangs. PSHT and 7/7 – just two of the many – are unlike any gangs I have met before. One of them is a 30,000-strong fighting force, the other has members who think they are literally invincible. The gangs claim to be apolitical, but the explosion of violence I witnessed on my last night there proved to me that this was not the case. In East Timor politics and gangsterism seemed to be inextricably linked, and until the politicians do something about the poverty in which so many people live, this will continue to be the case. As I write this I am soon to return for the wedding of our guide José. I hope I will see some sort of progress there, but only time will tell.

High on a mountain outside Dili there is a huge statue – twenty-seven metres high – of Jesus. It was built by Indonesian settlers in the mid-1990s, and is known as Christ the King. It's an impressive sight as it looks austerely yet benevolently out to sea. And yet when it was built it was said by many East Timorese that Jesus looks out over the ocean because he can't bear to see what is happening in their country. They knew, even then, that it was becoming a gangster's paradise. And unless men like President Ramos-Horta — who at the time of writing is happily still the president, despite the attempt on his life — have their way, unless grass-roots attempts to lessen the power of the gangs such as the refuge run by José start to work, it seems to me that it could be a long time before Jesus will want to turn and look with pleasure upon this devout, beautiful, desperate island.

4. Los Angeles

The prisons of California are home to some of the most dangerous, violent men in America. A good proportion of them will never be released. They live lives of grinding monotony; some of them barely ever see the sunshine. They've been taken off the streets and out of play.

At least, that's the idea.

The reality is quite different, because LA is home to a varied culture of prison gangs – highly organized groups of criminals whose word is law and whose methods of enforcement are brutal and shockingly effective. They are also surprisingly ingenious, as I was to find out when I investigated them. These people aren't stupid. Make that mistake with them and the chances are that you'll meet a sticky end. Sticky like blood, if you get my meaning. I've been to LA a number of times now, and perhaps more than any place I've ever been to, I've always felt that if I didn't show the proper respect to the people I was with, things could have turned nasty.

What is most intriguing about the prison gangs of LA is that their influence does not stop at the walls of whatever institution they happen to be in. They pass instructions down to the street gangs – who carry them out, if they know what's good for them. It seems like a weird situation. What on earth drives a young street gang member to carry out the orders of men serving 300-year sentences, men who will never, ever see the light of day again? And how do these people maintain their grip on power when they're locked in a cell for twenty-three hours of the day?

The answers to these questions – and others – came to me over a period of years and over several visits. I travelled to California some time ago to investigate the skinhead prison gangs of Orange County. What I learned on that trip opened my eyes and introduced me to the goings-on in the prisons of this violent part of America. I have also spent time with the Bloods and the Crips – probably the most famous gangs in LA, if not the world. Most recently, I went to California to find out about a Latino gang whose influence on the streets was beginning to eclipse even that of the Bloods and Crips: La eMe, the Mexican Mafia. La eMe is one of the oldest prison gangs in the United States. Estimating its size is an imprecise science: it's guesstimated that there are between twenty and thirty full members with the authority to order killings – the vast majority of whom are in prison – while there are thought to be thousands of associates from Hispanic gangs on the streets who carry out these killings. Of the Hispanic gangs on the streets of LA, the most important to La eMe are those that they call the Sureños.

Prison gangs, then, are big business. I wanted to find out more about them. To do so meant putting myself and the film crew bang in the centre of some of the most dangerous streets in America. I was going to have to talk to some of the most unpredictable men in the world and I was even going to have to track down an old friend . . .

To look at it, you would never imagine that Orange County is the sort of place where racist skinhead gangs proliferate. It's the richest county in California, a surfer's paradise and home to Disneyland – although even without Mickey Mouse it would be a top tourist destination with its sandy beaches, yacht harbours and golf courses. But it's also home to racist gangs whose level of violence is on a par with anything

I have ever seen. The two main gangs in Orange County when I visited were the Nazi Lowriders and Public Enemy Number 1, or PEN1 (pronounced peni), as they are more commonly known. The Lowriders – named after the low-rider cars favoured by Mexicans – were a Mexican Nazi gang, PEN1 a white Nazi gang. What they had in common, though, was that they were both brutal and ruthless. They operated an extreme code of silence that meant it was going to be very difficult to get close to them.

I had seen footage of white-power rallies and gatherings in the state of California. It wasn't something to make the average American proud. At one rally a man told a joke: 'How do you get a nigger out of a tree?' 'Cut the rope.' It gave me an idea of what to expect from these people. And I had seen gruesome stills of two PEN1 members who had made the mistake of speaking to the media. They were dead, of course, but the horrific bruises all over their faces and bodies told of the treatment they had received before the inevitable came. I rather hoped the people I was investigating wouldn't take such a dim view of *my* interest in them.

In order to get close to these skinhead gangs, I hooked up with the police department's gang enforcement team in an area of Orange County called Costa Mesa. The team showed me photographs of some of the gang members they had in their sights: suffice to say that they didn't look like the kind of people you'd want to invite round to tea. Their heads were shaved, their skin was tattooed – they were big ugly-looking guys who didn't use their muscles to chop logs. It was people like this that we were going to try and find when I went on patrol with my new police acquaintances that night.

Our destination was the Mesa Motor Inn. Take my advice: if you're passing through the area, give this place a miss –

especially if your skin's not lily white. It's a kind of halfway house between prison and the streets for skinhead gang members. Most of the people staying here were on parole and none of them were pleased to see us, particularly not the guy who had just taken a hit of crystal meth, which seemed at the time to be the drug of choice in these groups. But despite the obvious signifiers – the shaved heads, the tattoos – none of the residents of the Mesa Motor Inn were willing to admit to belonging to a racist gang. The reason for this was clear: if you get convicted of a crime and it can be proved that it was racially motivated, you face a much stiffer penalty. The people I was meeting weren't stupid; they were keeping quiet in front of the cops and the cameras. One guy, however, was prepared to admit that although he claimed not to be part of a racist gang, he shared their beliefs. It was quite clear that militant racism was alive and well at the Mesa Motor Inn.

It wasn't confined to this dodgy motel, however. During the course of my stay in Orange County I met some pretty unsavoury types. Tom Metzger was one of them. A former member of the Ku Klux Klan, he subsequently founded an organization called White Aryan Resistance. He runs his own radio show promoting race hate and his website currently has a number of games to download including Kaboom! The Suicide Bombing Game, Border Patrol – Don't Let Those Spics Cross Our Border and Watch Out Behind You, Hunter – Shoot the Fags Before They Rape You!

Lovely bloke.

And I met the lead singer of a band called Extreme Hatred, Marty Cox. Never was a band so aptly named. Their album covers display images of Jewish corpses, and he openly admitted that if any non-whites attended one of their gigs, they'd get beaten up. I asked him if he thought his anti-Semitic lyrics were offensive to Jews. 'I hope so,' he replied. Jews, he explained, were offensive to *him* because of their lies about the Holocaust. Sure, people died, but it was a war. People die in wars. Get over it. A fine, upstanding example of the pure-bred Aryan race.

People like Tom Metzger and Marty Cox add fuel to the racist fire and I've no doubt that they are admired by white-power groups all over America. But they're not gang members themselves. I was going to find it far more difficult to locate a racist gangster prepared to talk to me on the record. When I *was* finally granted an interview with a convicted PEN1 leader, I was left in no doubt as to the level of violence to which they were accustomed. Such was the secrecy surrounding these gangs that we were not allowed to take the cameras into the interview at the Santa Anna House of Correction, where he was being held. It didn't matter – the tape recording was compelling enough.

I asked him how PEN1 operated. 'There's a lot of different things that go on,' he told me. 'There's drug distribution, murder for hire, furtherance of our political views.'

And what, exactly, were those views?

'PEN1 is a white-power gang. We're about producing a good future for our white kids. There are eighty-eight precepts on how to live – what not to do, how to speak, how to treat people. Some guys in prison get red braces tattooed on their body, which represents that they killed a black guy. I've got 187 – that represents murder – tattooed on me. That's the penal code for murder.'

So did that mean he had committed a murder?

'I don't know if I want to go into that,' he told me with a knowing look. 'But if you wanted to kill someone, how hard is it? Shave yourself down, put some grease on and some baby powder, put some clothes on, get yourself a

Glock with an interchangeable barrel, kill the person, toss the gun off the speedway and it's done. That's how easy it is, but there's not too many people with the *cojones* to talk about it.'

No indeed. And far be it for me to make any accusations, but it certainly sounded like I was listening to a description of murder by someone who was fairly intimately acquainted with the process. I asked him why everyone was so reluctant to talk. If these people were gang members – hard, tough men – why didn't they want to speak to the likes of us?

'Well,' the PEN1 leader told me, 'the last guy who did what I'm doing got killed for it.'

Sounded like a pretty good reason to me. But didn't that make him nervous? Didn't he think that the same people who had killed the last guy might try and do the same to him.

'No,' he said with a quiet, understated confidence. 'I don't. I'm much higher up. I have a big reputation in prison.'

It was a revealing interview. The PEN1 commander was firmly behind bars and alluding to the fact that in prison there was a gang power structure and a hierarchy. As I investigated further, I learned that prison, far from being where the racist gangs of California are suppressed and removed from circulation, was in fact a hotbed of gang activity. PEN1 and the Nazi Lowriders positively thrived in jail, and from what I could tell they used their prison cells as centres of command. It seemed difficult to believe that they could still wield power on the streets despite being incarcerated, but the more I learned about these gangs, the more that seemed to be the case.

The Nazi Lowriders and PEN1 were affiliated to each other and had one other thing in common: the Aryan Brotherhood, a highly organized prison gang claiming Irish roots that was the dominant white-power force in the US. The Nazi Lowriders had in the past been used as muscle for the Brotherhood, carrying out their commands on the street. In fact, the AB – the Brand as they sometimes call themselves – had, even from their prison cells, been the real power behind all the white gangs for some time. This was confirmed by another PEN1 member who was finally persuaded to speak to us. 'The Brand,' he told me, 'are the cream of the crop. That's where everyone wants to go and they will do their bidding – kill for them. The people who are calling the shots, they don't care about themselves, they don't care about others; they're never getting out.'

So if you're told to kill someone by the Aryan Brotherhood, you have to carry that out?

'Correct.'

And if you don't?

'You die. If you don't do something that you're told to do, the same thing that you're told to do's going to happen to you.'

That sounded to me like a pretty powerful incentive. It was also clear that if I wanted to find out more about American white-power gangs, I would have to visit a prison. I asked my source which facility would be the most fruitful for my purposes.

He replied without a moment's thought. 'Pelican Bay,' he said. 'Pelican Bay. That's the cream of the crop.'

Pelican Bay State Prison. It's not a place you want to end up. It's a 'supermax' prison facility situated on 275 acres near the California–Oregon state line. Surrounded on all sides by forest, it's 370 miles from San Francisco and 750 miles from Los Angeles. Put simply, it's a long way from anywhere and there's a reason for this.

Getting to Pelican Bay is difficult even if you're a criminal. You have to have done something pretty bad indeed, and you have to show a penchant for continuing to do so. And for a lad from Essex and his camera crew, getting there proved to be a nightmare. We had to apply for permission to visit months in advance, as it took this much time for our security clearances to be processed. To make things more difficult, we had chosen to visit when America was in post-9/11 security lockdown. We were due to fly to northern California from LAX airport, where of course we were subjected to the inevitable internal security measures that had been put in place. As a result of practically having to strip down for the security guards, it was looking likely that we were going to miss our plane – and therefore our window at the prison.

Our camera crew finally got on to the aircraft while the American director and I removed our socks and were rechecked for explosives for a third time. And by now our gate had closed. It was too much for the director, who went into full-blown John McEnroe mode. '*They're* on the plane!' he yelled. 'Why can't *we* get on the plane?'

The airline lady shook her head firmly. 'I'm sorry, sir. The gate is closed. We cannot let you on the plane now.'

He ignored the woman, walked straight past her and strode through the security doors towards the plane.

Bad move.

We knew we were going to a prison that day, but what we didn't know was how close we would come to sampling the Californian incarceration system at rather closer quarters. The security guards of course didn't care that the director was American. It didn't matter at the time if you were black, green, orange or yellow – everyone was a suspect, and unless we did some pretty fast talking, we were going to jail. I had to plead – literally – for us to be allowed to go on our way. Somehow we managed it, but it took an entire day and trips out of the state via three different airports to reach the forbidden environs of Pelican Bay.

The region around the prison is like Cornwall on acid. They say everything in America is bigger; well it was certainly the case here. The 'pebbles' on the beach were the size of buses; the trees in the forest were the giant redwoods that you can literally drive a truck through – if they obstruct the road, an enormous hole is cut into them to make an arch through which vehicles can pass. Everything seemed magnified, as though you were looking at it through a telescope. It's beautiful in its way – I remember watching the sun going down over the mountains and being captivated by the reds and mauves – and it's rugged and wild. You get the sense of being a long way from civilization. Pelican Bay isn't isolated like Alcatraz, but as we headed through the forest I certainly remember thinking that I wouldn't particularly want to be on the run here, with nothing but the clothes on my back, having escaped from jail.

Not that anyone ever *has* escaped. People have tried, but no one's ever come close.

Pelican Bay opened in 1989. Its purpose was to house the ever-growing number of maximum-security and high-risk inmates in the Californian prison system. It was originally intended to contain around 2,500 prisoners; today that number is more like 3,500. Almost all of these are classed as Level 4: maximum security.

The Bay is a prison within a prison. Half of it holds 'regular' maximum-security prisoners in a general population. These inmates have access to limited periods of time in outdoor exercise areas. This might not sound like a great luxury, but when you're banged up for most of the day it certainly is. The other half of the prison, however, contains the feature for which Pelican Bay has earned most of its notoriety. The Secure Housing Unit, or SHU (pronounced shoe), is separated from the rest of the prison by electric fencing and barren wasteland. It was the SHU that I was interested in. This is where they put those prisoners who have a history of violence whilst inside prison; it's where they put the people they can't control; and, crucially for my purposes, it's where they put lifers who are identified as being members of prison gangs.

Conditions in the SHU make life in the general prison seem positively cushy. Instead of the luxury of an outdoor exercise area, you get the 'dog run'. This is a concrete room about twenty feet by ten. There is no ceiling, but the grim, stained concrete walls are about three storeys high. If you want to scale them, you need to be Spiderman – and you need to be invisible to the ever-present security camera that is constantly fixed on you as you exercise. Inmates of the SHU get no more than an hour a day in the dog run, and that's all the exercise they're allowed. Despite that, it's remarkable how fit some of them remain.

When I went to Pelican Bay, there were three separate runs for three separate gangs: the Aryan Brotherhood, the Black Guerrilla Family and the Mexican Mafia. While I was there, I discovered a great deal about what life in prison is like for gang members. It was an eye-opener, to say the least.

I learned that you could tell a great deal about a particular prison by examining the inmates' cells. In the SHU the cells are made from smoothed-down concrete. There are no sharp corners – it looks as if the room has been moulded or sculpted. There are two mattresses, two bunks and some bedclothes. In one corner is a small metal toilet. The doors are made of red metal, and have small perforations in them a little thicker than a biro. This enables the prison staff to check on the inmates without having to open the door.

Some of these doors have sheets of perspex placed in front of them. The reason for this was explained to me: some of the inmates are 'sprayers' – people who spray harmful liquids on other prisoners or guards who walk past their perforated doors. I wondered what 'harmful liquids' meant and I was soon put right. All prisoners have the right to a roll-on deodorant in their cell. The liquid in this contains a small amount of alcohol, which is used for all sorts of purposes. Some inmates flavour it with fruit and drink it – hardly Chateau Latour '69, but you've got to work with what you've got – but it is also used as a solvent to mix with whatever bodily effluents they decide to spray their chosen enemy with. Blood, semen, piss, shit – any of these can be and are mixed with the liquid from the deodorants and sprayed through the holes in the cell doors. The purpose is to cover the victim in the stuff.

So, those members of the SHU population who are designated as sprayers have their doors blocked with clear plastic, but most don't. That doesn't mean to say that the perforations have no other use, and what I learned about the way in which they are used is a testament to the ingenuity, persistence and patience of the prison population. The inmates are not allowed biros, as the plastic barrels have, in the past, been used as blowpipes. But they are allowed the inside section – the ballpoint and the plastic tube of ink – in order to write letters home. It was explained to me that they remove the plastic coating around the ballpoint and then, at night, sharpen the point against the concrete of the cell using soap as a lubricant in much the same way as oil is used on a whetstone. Over time – and you have to remember that time is the one thing these people have – it becomes sharp enough to use as a weapon.

By itself, however, the sharpened biro is difficult to use. What is required is a crossbow of sorts. Given the materials at hand, you might think that making such a thing is impossible, but once more the resourcefulness of these people is astonishing. Paper and envelopes are allowed in cells, again so that the inmates can write letters home. They also have another use, however. The paper is chewed down into a kind of papier mâché. This is then mixed with the gum from the flap of the envelope to make a very hard substance, a bit like balsa wood. This papier mâché has a number of uses. Some inmates fashion little hooks that can be stuck (again with the envelope gum) above the door. They then hang a sheet over the perforated door so that they can masturbate, or do whatever it is they want to do, in private. Less benignly, the papier mâché is also used to make the body of a crossbow. The inmates take a piece of newspaper, roll it up very tightly and cover it with adhesive and alcohol. The resulting tube is incredibly hard. While I was in Pelican Bay I was shown one of these things. They're about thirteen or fourteen inches long and as tough as bamboo. There's a little hole at one end through which the sharpened biro is placed. All that's missing now is some form of elastic to make the string of the crossbow.

Around the top of your underpants and your socks there's a thin band of elastic. This can be unpicked. What you get is a mass of extremely thin, insubstantial elastic. It can be glued together to form a much stronger band. It's a slow, painstaking process – just making a single crossbow can take a year – but it isn't like the inmates of the SHU have any other pressing matters. They just bide their time and, assuming the fledgling crossbow doesn't get clocked by one of the warders, sooner or later they have a dangerous weapon. And one that can be fired from inside the cell through the perforations in the door.

Once you have your crossbow, all you need to decide is who you're going to hit – and where. Over the years both warders and prisoners have been injured and even killed by this means. In order to inflict maximum damage, the inmates spend time learning the exact eye height of their potential victim so that the dart can be fired directly into the eyeball. When I was in Pelican Bay I saw one cell that had a number of different eye heights marked by the door. Clearly that cell's occupant had a lot of enemies.

Anything made of metal is a massively sought-after piece of contraband in the SHU. Every morning the metal flush handles on the in-cell toilets are checked to make sure they haven't been removed in order to be used for more sinister purposes. Nail clippers, I learned, are like gold dust. The metal from which they are made is supposed to be stronger than the metal in the doors. This means that they can be used to cut away tiny pieces from the door. Obviously this takes a very long time, but again, when you know you're never getting out of there . . .

Illegal items such as nail clippers and the like clearly cannot simply be brought in and out of the SHU, and so the inmates, as they do in many other prisons, use the well-worn trick of keestering: inserting objects into your rectal cavity to avoid detection. It's a technique usually used to smuggle drugs (the drugs themselves are sometimes referred to as keester eggs – not quite what the Easter bunny had in mind), but it seems that the rectal cavity is more adaptable than most people realize, and it's used to transport all sorts of other things. I'm not sure *I'd* want to secrete a pair of nail clippers up there, but maybe that's just me.

Another prison term I was told about was 'tossing the salad', which sounds like a healthy option but I can assure you is not good for your palate or your digestive system. To be a salad tosser means that you are forced (unless you're into that kind of thing) to lick the backside of Mr Big after he has defecated while relieving him manually. Again, another reason not to end up in prison.

The more I learned about what went on inside Pelican Bay, the more I began to understand just how a gang might put their hands on the materials they needed to maintain their violent grip on power within the prison walls. And the more people I spoke to, the more it became clear that the Aryan Brotherhood were a prison gang to be reckoned with. The AB has a long history. Up until the 1960s most prisons in the United States were segregated by race. Desegregation was gradually introduced, but that didn't stop inmates from dividing along racial lines, and it is thought that the first faction of the Brand was formed in San Quentin State Prison in 1964. It has close ties with various biker gangs.

The Aryan Brotherhood, as their name suggests, espouse Nazi ideology, so as you can imagine they're an extremely pleasant bunch of lads. Naziism has become a cult for them, and every aspect of their lives is imbued with symbols and beliefs relating to Adolf Hitler and the Nazis. For example, as I had learned from the PEN1 leader in Santa Anna, they have eighty-eight rules by which they live their lives. As with the gang I had met in Poland, the number eighty-eight is significant because it represents the eighth letter of the alphabet repeated. HH. *Heil Hitler.* Similarly, a common punishment meted out by the Aryan Brotherhood is being punched in the face eighteen times. One eight: AH. Adolf Hitler. Unpleasant, but actually quite mild by the standards of the Brand. It's a 'blood in, blood out' gang: you have to kill to become a member, and you only leave when you die. Members' skins are plastered with Nazi iconography, tattoos being, for them as for many other gangs, an integral part of their identity. The fact that they can get tattooed while inside is another reminder of the ingenuity of the prison population in the SHU. Clearly inmates are not allowed the proper machinery with which to draw tattoos; what they are allowed, however, are old-style cassette recorders. They use these to make tattooing machines by connecting a small piece of guitar string to the spools and using the fast-forward button to make it spin round quickly. This is then dipped into biro ink. It's incredibly ingenious and the artwork that they produce using these machines is absolutely amazing, albeit in a grotesque kind of way. I met one man who had a diamond of swastikas from his neck down to his pectorals, then back down to his stomach. Inside that he had a Teutonic knight brandishing a sword. Another Brand associate had detailed pictures of Eva Braun and Himmler on his back, as well as a full Nazi death skull. Grizzly, but undeniably impressive under the circumstances.

When I arrived at Pelican Bay I was given a stab jacket – mandatory dress for anyone entering the SHU. Nobody in the Aryan Brotherhood was prepared to speak to me – their wall of silence was impenetrable. In some ways this wasn't such a bad thing – the AB sounded like a very scary bunch. I heard a story of one of their number who killed his cell mate. It made no difference to him, as he was going to be in the SHU for the rest of his life, but he was pleased he'd done it because it meant he'd get extra food for a couple of days before the warders worked out that the unpleasant smell coming from the other bunk wasn't down to poor personal hygiene. Why he wanted extra portions of the foul 'donkey dick' sausage and sauerkraut the AB were served,

God only knows; but it was a cautionary tale for anyone who wanted to mess with the Brand.

At the time I visited Pelican Bay the federal government was cracking down on the Aryan Brotherhood using a law available to them known as RICO. RICO stands for Racketeer Influenced and Corrupt Organizations Act, although some people claim it's a sly reference to a gangster movie called *Little Caesar*, in which the lead criminal character is named Rico. RICO states that if a person commits any two of thirty-five crimes within a period of ten years, they are liable to increased penalties. It's a statute primarily aimed at organized crime – indeed it was recently used to convict members of the notorious Gambino Mafia family. As a result, there seemed to be a certain amount of uncertainty about the future of the Aryan Brotherhood. If RICO removed those on the streets who carried out their orders, would the organization survive? There was much talk about who would take the Brand's place if the RICO actions were successful in their aim. Some people's money was on PEN1, others backed the Nazi Lowriders. Whatever the final outcome, it was clear that there was a good deal of infighting in the ranks of the gangs at Pelican Bay.

Although I was unable to speak to current members of the AB, I did secure an interview with a handful of former members who had refused to comply with the gang's instructions to kill certain of its own members as a result of this infighting. These men had to be kept isolated from the main body of AB prisoners because otherwise they would undoubtedly have been killed. Their opinion was quite definite: the Aryan Brotherhood was in control. Top of the heap. The idea that PEN1 or anyone would replace them was ridiculous.

Other people told me different things. But one thing was

clear: from within their prison cells the Aryan Brotherhood wielded a great deal more power than you might expect from a bunch of guys who were never going to see the light of day again. And five years on, when I returned to LA to investigate some of the other gangs in that part of America, it is worth noting that despite the indictment of their leading members under the RICO act, the Brand is still going strong. Although they make up less than one per cent of the jail population, they are responsible for 26 per cent of the murders in the federal prison system.

This time I wasn't here to speak to Californian skinheads. For forty years the gang capital of the world has been dominated by the black gangs the Bloods and the Crips. Word had reached me, however, that their dominance was being challenged by Hispanics. I wanted to find out if there was any truth in this and to see if there were any similarities with the gangs I had encountered on my trip to Orange County.

Los Angeles is a two-sided place. On the one hand, it's glamorous and affluent – famous for its thriving film and television industries, home to the Hollywood stars and the biggest city in California, the seventh-largest economy on the planet. On the flip side are some astonishing statistics. The city is home to 700 gangs. In 2007 there was a gang-related murder every other day. In February 2008 there were just under 2,000 violent crimes committed. For generations there have been battles between the Bloods and the Crips and clearly things are not getting any better.

Of the two gangs, the Crips are the older. It was formed in 1969 by two black teenagers, Raymond Washington and Stanley Tookie Williams. The gang was originally named the Baby Avenues and then renamed itself the Avenue Cribs –

it took on the name Cribs because its members were so young. Whether it became the Crips because of a misspelling or because some of its members used to carry canes, as though they were crippled, is a matter of debate. What is beyond question is that the Crips became hugely popular throughout southern Los Angeles and it wasn't long before Crips outnumbered other gangs by five to one. By 1971 the gang had spread throughout the whole of Los Angeles. Gradually the Crips became a loosely connected network of sets rather than one single gang. It was also in 1971 that a Crip set which called itself the Piru Street Boys was formed. As time passed, tensions started to show between this gang and the other Crip sets. In the mid-70s the Piru Street Boys joined forces with various other anti-Crip gangs and formed the Bloods.

Perhaps the most notorious gang hatred in the world had been born.

Like most gangs, the Bloods and the Crips evolved their own signs and styles. The Crips developed a tendency to wear blue; the Bloods wore red. They each developed their own ways of speaking. They carved out their own turf, and soon gang warfare had become so entrenched in the street culture of Los Angeles there seemed little likelihood of it ever going away.

The hub of this gang activity is the city of Compton in southern Los Angeles. It's the front line between the warring gangs. I don't doubt that the inhabitants of Compton would hate anyone calling the place where they live a ghetto. But that's what it is. It has a homicide rate eight times higher than the national average, the vast majority of which are gang-related killings. A recent amnesty offered the inhabitants of Compton $100 to hand over any firearms they possessed, and there are more gangster rap songs written about Compton than anywhere else. 'Compton' has become a euphemism for anything related to gangs. Before we ventured on to the streets of this gang-riddled area of LA we were given one piece of sound advice: there are certain areas where you don't stop at a red light after it gets dark. Just drive through. It's safer that way.

In the middle of all this are the police. In 2000 the Compton Police Department was disbanded. Local law enforcement was handed over to the Los Angeles Sheriff's Department. When I arrived in LA, it was the LASD that was my first port of call. In order for me to get some sort of idea of the extent of the problem, they invited me on a night patrol of Compton.

My contacts were straight out of an American cop drama. The sheriff's department does not get the kind of publicity and the glamour that seems to have rubbed off on the LAPD, but Deputies Mark Sannagauer and Ben Torres of the LASD's specialized gang unit were the real deal. You could put them in their own show tomorrow and they'd hit the top of the ratings. Like all good police partners, they've become friends – their kids play Little League together, they have barbecues at each other's house at the weekends and of course they always watch each other's backs. And for a Compton cop there's a lot of back-watching to be done. Mark and Ben both carry Beretta pistols as well as tiny .38 revolvers that fit into a little wallet. They're armed to the teeth and you get the impression that they live double lives – one filled with wives and taking the kids to school and barbecues, the other filled with gunfire, dead bodies and gang warfare. I asked Ben how often he used his gun.

'What do you mean?' he asked me. 'To shoot people?'

'Not necessarily,' I said.

He shrugged. 'I use my gun every day,' he told me. And

when I finally saw him in action, I realized what he meant. The LASD gang department use their guns like a sheep farmer uses a sheepdog. Step out on an operation with these guys and they don't have their firearms slung in a holster. The moment they're out of their car, the gun is out, like an extension of their hand. They use it to tell people what to do and where to go, to herd them from one place to another. It's a tool of the trade and without it they couldn't do their job.

The first thing they did was show me a map of Compton divided into gang territories. There were, I was told, sixty-eight active gangs in Compton alone. That's seven gangs per square mile. It struck me that each area was delineated by perfectly straight lines – a result of the American grid system of town planning, a phenomenon that helps gangs to thrive. In the UK, for example, a gang might define itself by the slightly amorphous criterion of which area of London it comes from, or which estate, but in Compton it's much easier for them to mark out distinct boundaries. North of one street might belong to one gang, who would claim the right to sell drugs and run protection rackets there; south of that street might belong to another. And it's on the street corners, where the territories of up to four separate gangs can meet, that the violence most often takes place. The grid system also divides rich and poor in such a way that the gulf between the two is thrown into much sharper relief. In certain parts of downtown LA you can find barriers running down the middle of the road, two-storey-high iron bars with spikes on the top that separate one neighbourhood from another. On one side of the iron bars you'll have streets full of drug pedlars and shoot-outs; on the other side of the road you've got massive houses that look like they've been airlifted out of New Hampshire or some other affluent area.

Wealth and luxury on one side; poverty and murder on the other. It's no wonder that the tension between the two often spills out on to the streets.

The offices where I met Mark and Ben included a room in the basement where they kept gear that had been confiscated from the gangs – a shrine to gangsterism. It was explained to me that LA gang members, being so territorial, generally wanted to wear clothes that made it clear where they were from. I was shown a red baseball cap with a white W emblazoned on the front. It had nothing to do with LA – this was the team cap of the Washington Nationals – but it had been confiscated from a member of a Blood set called the Westside Pirus. Red is the gang colour of the bloods, and the W had been appropriated because it was the initial of their gang name. All over the walls of this room were photographs of gang members. I was shown one picture of a mother at her son's funeral. As she stood over the coffin with her family around her, she was throwing a Blood gang sign – P for Piru. The fact that a grieving mother could do this somehow spoke volumes about the situation.

Elsewhere in the room there were T-shirts hanging on the wall. Words and phrases were written on these T-shirts, but I noticed that the letters C and B were crossed out. Mark and Ben told me why. You'd never get a Blood using the letter C if he or she could avoid it; similarly a Crip would try not to use B. So it is that two new dialects have sprung up on the streets of Los Angeles. A Blood wouldn't talk about Compton, he'd talk about Bompton; he wouldn't go for a cup of coffee, he'd go for a bup of boffee. And a Crip wouldn't talk about bunting, he'd talk about . . . Well, you get the idea. It sounds almost comical – it certainly sounds difficult to keep up – but the Bloods and the Crips speak their dialects with a genuine fluency.

Of course, it's when the gangs stop talking that you need to worry – because that's when they start shooting. Mark and Ben took me to a ballistics centre for the city of Los Angeles to show me some of the hardware they were up against on the streets. Most of the weapons are destroyed unless they're needed for a court case, but they keep a single copy of every gun they confiscate so that they know what they're dealing with. It's a formidable arsenal. I was shown a military shotgun that could destroy a Range Rover without much trouble; certainly it didn't fire the kind of shotgun pellets you'd use to bring wood pigeons down with, but the kind that will take down people and body armour. I was also handed an AK-47 with a bayonet on the end. As the cops told me rather succinctly, 'You're not hunting ducks with that thing.' These were military-grade weapons – definitely not the sort of hardware you wanted to come face to face with on the streets.

In order to be able to keep up with the heavily armed gang members, the LASD has its own wide-ranging arsenal. Part of this arsenal is a gangs vehicle containing all sorts of weaponry that that they can take out with them on raids. The equipment this thing packed seemed more suitable for the military than a police force. Among the weapons was a Stingball grenade. Based on the classic fragmentation grenade, the Stingball contains a store of 32-calibre rubber pellets. There is a short delay on the grenade before it explodes. It's a distraction device and a deterrent – the effect is to make the target feel as if they are coming under considerably more fire than they really are, lead rather than rubber, and they immediately fall to the ground – but in any case I'm not sure *I'd* want to take a hit from one of those rubber pellets. I was also shown a shotgun that fired little beanbags full of pellets – these will impact their target with considerable force, but the pellets won't actually enter the body. And finally I saw a Colt M4 carbine – a serious piece of kit which, having been in Afghanistan, I knew was used in most of the major war zones around the world by the US army. The sergeant who was showing me most of this equipment explained that, while he obviously wouldn't pull a weapon like this for a traffic violation, there were definitely circumstances when it would be a necessary tool. But he also added that no matter how well armed the department appeared to be, the guns they were facing out on the street were far superior to anything the police had. 'We're always playing catch-up,' he told me.

Having seen the kind of weaponry both sides in this war were packing, it was with a certain amount of apprehension that I climbed into a police patrol car after dark and headed out into the streets of one of the most dangerous parts of America. Compton is very urban, very industrial. Railway lines run through it, a mesh of pylons runs above it, and most of the buildings are single-storey, breeze-block-type affairs with linked fences outside and bars across the windows. In the middle of all this low-rise housing is a justice house, several storeys high, that seems to dominate the landscape. On the top of the building is a camera that is programmed to point itself in the direction of any gun-fire. You get the impression the justice house exists to remind the inhabitants of this part of town that the law is always there. Whether it succeeds or not is questionable; certainly the crime statistics don't seem to suggest it does. But high-tech security cameras or not, one thing is clear about Compton just from a glance: salubrious it ain't.

It didn't take long for us to come across a gang. We were in a Blood area of Compton and a bunch of guys was on a street corner, rolling dice, smoking weed and generally just chilling. Our patrol pulled over and Mark and Ben got out of the car, Berettas at the ready. The gang members didn't look surprised to see them; nor did they look bothered when my escorts started searching them for drugs and guns. The deputies were mainly looking for large quantities of narcotics, but in this instance all they found was a small quantity of marijuana. They decided to let the gang go, but as we prepared to leave we started talking to a gang member who called himself Ricky 4. He proudly showed us one of his gang tattoos – a highly ornate figure 4 on the back of his hand – and he was wearing a pirate's patch over his right eye. My escorts commented to him that he wasn't wearing the patch last time they saw him – clearly he was a pretty familiar face to the cops. 'No,' he said with a whisper of a smile. 'I got shot in the face April twenty-third.'

There was something chilling about the way Ricky imparted this information – as though it was nothing to write home about. It happened when he was walking out of a nightclub, and not for the first time it was brought home to me how many people actually survive being shot these days. I wanted to know, of course, who had done this to him. Ricky wasn't going to name names, but Mark and Ben were able to shed some light on the matter. Back at the police station I had asked them about the demographics of the gangs in Compton. It was explained to me that whereas traditionally it was an area where black gangs predominated, of late there had been a shift in the population and now Compton was made up of 50 per cent black, 50 per cent Hispanic. The area where we were now was a black neighbourhood caught in the middle of two Hispanic areas. And from what the police were telling me, the Hispanics weren't taking any prisoners.

So was there really a race war going on between the blacks

and the Latinos? My police escorts were emphatic in their response. 'Yes,' they told me, 'without a doubt. You'll have a black gang, and you'll immediately know when a black gang member is shot that it was a Hispanic rival gang. The rival gang will yell out their gang name or throw a gang sign as they shoot them. They're letting these guys know, "You just got shot at by us. We're not afraid of you. We shot at you and we're not afraid to tell you who we are."'

How, I wondered, did it all start?

'They say it's a drug rip-off that they did years ago. The blacks sell drugs but don't pay any taxes to anybody in a Hispanic area.' It sounded pretty vague to me, a vendetta whose origin – like that of most vendettas – was long forgotten. One thing was clear though. 'It all comes back to money. If my gang's going to sell drugs, I don't want a black gang on the next block selling the same kind of drugs, because what if my customers go to him? It's bad for business.'

Bad for business. Like I'd seen in so many places before, it all came down to the green.

The Latino population of Los Angeles has been increasing since the early 1990s. Today for every black person in LA there are five Latinos. They are often referred to pejoratively as 'wetbacks', the implication being that their backs are still wet from crossing the Rio Grande – the river that forms a natural barrier between Mexico and Texas. Call someone a wetback and you're saying they're an illegal immigrant, but what a lot of people fail to remember is that a lot of Hispanic people have lived in California for hundreds of years. In fact, it's not called California for nothing. It's not called San Francisco for nothing. Same goes for Los Angeles and San Diego – the list of Hispanic place names could go on. The area, then known as Alta California, was colonized by the

Spanish in the mid-eighteenth century. After the Mexican–American war of 1846–8 California was ceded to the USA. And so when the Hispanics say, as they often do, 'We never moved, the border moved,' they've got a point. A lot of Latinos still perceive California as the land of the Mexicans and they have a very strong sense of their own heritage.

The Hispanic gangs of Compton and elsewhere in Los Angeles have a fearsome reputation. In order to find out just why, I decided to track down an old friend who I knew would be able to shed some light on the subject. Bloodhound is a Blood, and in many ways he's the reason I started investigating gangs in the first place. I originally met him several years ago when I was making a documentary on America's fascination with guns and he had struck me back then as a fascinating person. When I originally wrote about him, I protected his identity by calling him Hound Dog. Now he has agreed for his real name to be revealed. As a Blood living in an area entirely surrounded by Crips, he had been shot twenty-seven times. When he told me this I was sceptical so he showed me the entry and exit wounds. He counted them off one by one. Hearing Bloodhound talk was like listening to a man whose life was charmed, because the fact that his body was ravaged with bullet wounds (including one, eye-wateringly enough, in his testicles) meant he was incredibly lucky to be alive. As he was lying unconscious on the floor during one particularly brutal attack by a rival Crip gang, he was shot under the chin with a nine-millimetre pistol. The bullet removed the tip of his tongue, ripped out the side of his nose, re-entered through the top of his left eye socket and embedded itself in his forehead. Certainly one to tell the grandchildren – and amazingly, despite the unfortunate incident with his testicles, grandchildren don't appear to be an impossibility.

Meeting Bloodhound for the first time was an eye-opener. It made me realize that being in a gang was not about fast cars, faster women and loads of bling – the image that's sold to us by the culture of gangster rap. It's about a brutal, mean way of existence; it's about poverty and violence. While we were filming Bloodhound first time round, one of his friends was shot. He died two days later. Bloodhound knew it could easily have been him. We all knew it could easily have been him.

Bloodhound was an intelligent guy. Smart. Streetwise. You have to be to survive in a world like that. I knew that if anyone could tell me about a change in the balance of power in the LA gangs, Bloodhound was the man. We arranged to meet on a street corner where, coincidentally, he had previously been shot. Bloodhound was carrying his characteristic blood-red bandanna and it was good to see him. He looked older than the last time we met, but then we both did. We were both a little wiser and a little wider. In fact he couldn't have been much more than in his thirties, though by Blood standards that's practically geriatric. You don't have a very high life expectancy on the streets.

Bloodhound was like an elder statesman, and he certainly walked the streets as though he owned them. Truth was, however, he most decidedly did *not* own the ones we were heading towards. He was taking me to an area where he had been shot on several occasions. That meant Crip territory. He led me to a famous black-power mural and we conducted our interview there. Now, hanging on a famous Crip corner with a well-known Blood openly sporting his colours is not the best way I can think of to ensure a long and healthy life. I don't mind saying that I was kind of on edge as I chatted to my old friend.

I was used, I suppose, to his stories of attacks at the

hands of Crip gangs, but as we talked he told me that more recently he had been targeted by the Latinos. He explained what had happened. 'They put a pipe bomb inside my car and it was hooked up to the starter. My home boy cranked the engine. We didn't know it was a fucking bomb in there, so it blew up. My face was on fire for a minute, which doesn't sound long, but when your face is on fire, especially round your eyes . . .'

Actually, a minute was starting to sound like quite a long time.

Bloodhound continued: 'I'm trying to put it out, but it won't come out. I'm smothering it, putting my shirt over it but it still won't come out. So I slammed my face into a big bucket of water. It's been healing for about a year and I had to stay out of sunlight for a while.' The petrol had lifted the colour from his face — either that or he had been following in Michael Jackson's footsteps and somehow I didn't think that was quite his style.

Sunlight wasn't the only thing Bloodhound had to stay out of. He also had to move house. 'It was the smart thing to do,' he told me. 'Now where I stay is pretty much a secret. I don't let anyone know where I lay my head.'

As Bloodhound was speaking, a couple of cars pulled up alongside us. They were full of guys wearing Crip colours, and they didn't look like they were stopping to invite us to party with them. I found myself holding my breath. Thankfully, Bloodhound recognized one of them. 'It's all right, man,' he called out. 'We're just doing a film.'

The guys in the cars looked suspicious, but they drove off without saying much.

Bloodhound watched them go. 'Next time one of those cars comes back,' he said, 'we have to go. They're going down to tell the younger Crips that we're here. They'll come back and either tell us to get the fuck out, or shoot us.'

When you're talking to a man who's been shot as many times as Bloodhound, you tend to listen to him when he says it's all about to kick off.

We continued chatting. Bloodhound told me that the Latino gang that had targeted him were called 18 Street, a Mexican gang I had encountered before as they are also active in El Salvador. Before long I saw one of the cars returning. It drove past, spun round, then drove past again. Bloodhound checked out the driver. 'I don't know him,' he said tensely, 'and he's wearing colours.'

I looked at Bloodhound, whose Blood-red bandanna hanging from his jeans was like a beacon in this Crip part of town. 'I tell you what, mate,' I told him. 'I think we've been here long enough.'

Bloodhound nodded with a serious kind of expression. 'Yeah,' he said. 'We need to go.'

We left.

As we walked the streets, Bloodhound pointed out a lamp post. It was covered in gang graffiti and he explained that these are used as totem poles – markers to clarify which gang a particular street belongs to. The graffiti looked like a foreign language to me, but Bloodhound was able to translate it fluently. When your life depends on making sure you don't walk down the wrong street wearing the wrong clothes, I guess little things like that come to you pretty quickly.

Later, Bloodhound introduced us to a friend of his. His name was Stutterbox and as he told us, 'I'll be a Blood till I die.' Stutterbox's medical history was pretty varied, and it had culminated in an incident when he was waiting for a bus and some Crips came up to him. They started to diss Stutterbox, and in the fight that ensued one of the Crips pulled a gun and shot him in the side of the head. The bullet took the retina out of one eye and exited from the other. Stutterbox fell to the ground, unable to see and his face full of blood. While he was on the floor, they shot him another six times. God knows how he survived, but by some miracle there he was talking to me. Stutterbox was a bright man with a pleasant way of talking. He didn't seem at all bitter about the fact that he had lost his sight; in fact, he seemed pretty philosophical about the whole affair. He still carries a gun, but now he takes his son everywhere he goes. 'That way,' he told me, 'if anyone comes up to me, I pull out the gun; he tells me where to shoot, and I shoot!'

Stutterbox had a lot to say about the relationship between the black gangs and the Mexicans. One of the reasons he gave me for the animosity was that when the Mexican gangs first came to prominence they were bullied by the blacks in terms of the drug trade and who controlled the streets. Resentment built up and young Latinos grew up with that anger towards black gangs. The blacks were generally bigger than the Latinos and physically stronger, but the Latinos soon twigged that when you had a gun in your hand, it didn't matter how big you were. They were the underclass, they wanted to be the dominant force and now they knew how to do it. And the fact that the blacks were fighting each other as well as them only made things easier.

Bloodhound's experience with the car bomb had forced him to take a good look at his life, and he was doing what he could to put aside the gangster lifestyle. More than that, he was trying to do his bit towards ending the inter-gang warfare on the streets of LA. As a result, he had contact with a number of Crips. As I was really trying to get into the mindset of both black gangs, he agreed to set up a meet with a couple of them so I could listen to things from their side. It took three days. Bloodhound's instinct was that it was safer for us to bring the two Crips into his area than for us to risk venturing into Crip territory. Our contacts were two nineteen-year-olds, a boy called Baby Smurf and a girl called True Blue. Names like this are given to members by their gangs. Prefixes like Baby, Tiny or Small are quite common – our contact no doubt received his name because he resembled someone else in the gang whose gang name was Smurf. It's a way of identifying people, but it's also a way of introducing a sense of family.

Baby Smurf was a live wire. His face and head were completely covered by a blue Crips bandanna, so we smuggled him into Blood territory in our SUV. So far, everything seemed to be going OK. What we didn't count on, however, was that when we got him out of the car he would see a Blood sitting at the entrance to an apartment building and throw a gang sign at him. Short of putting a bullet in them, throwing a sign is about the most disrespectful thing you can do to a member of a rival gang. It's so much more than flicking a V-sign; more like a coded way of saying, 'Fuck you, I can rape your mamma.'

The Blood's reaction was instant. He stood up, but rather than come over and try to smack Baby Smurf in the face, he headed inside. We all knew that he wasn't going crying to his mummy; he was off to his apartment to fetch himself a gun.

Bloodhound stepped in immediately. He rushed up to the Blood and started calming him down, using his age and experience to ward off what was a potentially explosive situation. Luckily, he seemed to manage it. We watched as the young Blood, much calmer, walked away from the situation. We couldn't guarantee that he wouldn't be back, however, so we had to move Baby Smurf somewhere else. His ill-conceived gang sign had put his life in danger, and ours with it. That little incident taught me a lot about how quickly these incidents – arguments over nothing – can escalate. If it hadn't been for Bloodhound, Baby Smurf could well have been Dead Smurf, and we could easily have been caught in the crossfire.

We changed our location to a nearby car park. I didn't feel that happy about the place – there was only one way in and out, so if things turned bad we weren't going to get out of there in a hurry. But Bloodhound felt it would be safe and he was the guy with the local knowledge. In the car park we were joined by True Blue. True Blue was a fascinating character. She had become a Crip when her brother was shot dead on his way to school by a Blood. She was intelligent and articulate. In fact, she told me she wanted to become a lawyer. What the chances were of that now she wore a blue hood and the regulation blue bandanna over her face, I didn't know. Pretty slim, I would suggest. I was interested to know how deep her attachment to the Crips was. How far would she go to demonstrate her loyalty to the gang? What would she do for them?

'Whatever it takes,' she told me. It was a short response, but I knew what she was saying: she'd kill if she was ordered to. So it sounded like being a female in an LA gang was not that much different to being a male. I wondered if she agreed with that. Do the females have the same role to play as the males?

'Depends on the female,' True Blue told me laconically.

And what happens if a girl from one gang wanted to get together with a guy from another gang? I was guessing it wouldn't end up in a *West Side Story*-type dance routine, but did it ever happen?

'It happens,' she said, 'but it's trouble.'

Baby Smurf butted in. His take on the situation was a bit more robust. 'If I find one of my bitches fucking with a slob, I'm going to fuck the bitch up. I might just kill her then and there, depending on how we feel about her. If she's got some stripes or she got some stars, we ain't going to kill her, we just beat the bitch up and the homeys will gang-rape her. Other than that, we'll let the bitch slide, tell her to get off the 'hood.'

Leonard Bernstein, eat your heart out.

Entertaining as it would have been to listen to Baby Smurf's enlightened, pro-feminist views, I was here to talk about something different. I wanted to know if the Crips' experiences of Hispanic gangs were similar to Bloodhound's. I asked them what the situation was between the Latinos and the black gangs. True Blue told me that the severity of the situation depended on the area. She explained that it was much worse on the East Side, but that everywhere there was a racist divide: Latinos versus blacks. And that racism had spilled over into gangs.

Baby Smurf elaborated. From what I understood, it seemed that the warring factions might divide along lines of race, but that the root cause of the struggle was something more universal. 'Throughout the streets, everyone wants control of the drugs and the guns. Money is power.'

Just like everywhere else, the dollar is king.

It was time to get the Crips away from Blood turf. We bundled them back into the car and started driving. As we left Blood territory, however, Baby Smurf pointed something out to me that I had seen before in other gang areas. Hanging from the pylons high above us was a pair of trainers tied together by the laces. Baby Smurf explained what it meant. 'When somebody dies, they do that to represent their soul is here for ever. They throw their shoes up there to make sure they're still alive out here on these streets. Just recognition. You see, we don't get medals of honour. Most of us can't even afford tombstones. So we do that. That there means a Blood has been killed on this street.'

There was something poignant about Baby Smurf's explanation. It didn't matter to him that the trainers hanging above us used to belong to a Blood. He was moved by the very fact of their existence and he spoke eloquently and sadly about it. For all the brash talk about raping his bitches, he seemed to be describing a very human emotion, the need people all over the world – whether they're millionaires or paupers – have to remember their dead. It was a stark reminder that people in gangs may be poor, they may be violent, they may do and say things that are difficult for outsiders to understand. But strip all that away and you find people who are, at their core, very human.

You find people that aren't so different from you and me.

My spell in Compton, if nothing else, taught me one thing: despite the efforts of people like Bloodhound, the black gangs are intent on destroying each other. They're also under attack from the Hispanics among whom there seems to be no inter-gang fighting – or at least not to the same degree. It's not a good recipe for a long and healthy life. No wonder the balance of power is changing in favour of the Hispanics.

I'd heard about the shift in power from the black side of the trenches. But I wanted to get in deeper. I wanted to speak to the Latinos themselves. It wasn't going to be straightforward. The Mexican gangs are a secretive bunch. They don't like outsiders and they don't like publicity. Long and short of it was that a guy from the UK with a TV camera wasn't exactly going to float their boat. I had one contact, though. All I knew about him was that he was a Latino gang member by the name of Joker.

Joker agreed to meet me in a car park an hour's drive

from the city centre. It was midnight when we got there, and from the car park we were instructed to follow him to a far-flung part of LA. By the time we stopped – up a blind alley somewhere in Anaheim – there was a group of them waiting for us, wired and bolshie. To my left there was a wire fence, and over the fence, in the distance, was Disneyland. I had been told that in this part of LA more shootings happen during the evening between about nine and ten o'clock. Why? Because that's when the Disneyland firework displays happen. The sound of a Glock going off isn't so different to the sound of a rocket exploding over Cinderella's castle. Makes a pretty good cover. I looked at my watch. It was gone midnight now. Hopefully Cinderella would be fast asleep.

As I stepped out of the car telling them that I'd been told to ask for Joker, one of them waved a gun in my face. His finger was on the trigger and I didn't need to ask him if it was loaded. A tiny mistake from him and my gorgeous features would have been swiftly rearranged. They started hustling me a bit and then, from among them, one guy emerged. He wore a baseball cap on backwards and a white sports shirt. Joker was a big man. I told them I was there because I wanted to meet with the Mexican gangs, and they told me that they were Sureños – Mexican gang members from the south of Los Angeles. More than that, Joker didn't want to say. Not in front of the cameras and not until he had checked me out, verified that I was who I claimed to be. What he would do, however, was take me to meet some other southsiders, lads who would be less reticent about talking to us.

It was becoming clear that the Mexicans were far more secretive than the Bloods and Crips – they loved their covert rendezvous and secret locations. We piled back in the car and followed Joker and his boys back through Los Angeles for nearly an hour. We knew that the police had a habit of stopping vehicles travelling in convoys, so we did our best not to get spotted. It really wouldn't have done us much good at all to be caught in the company of a bunch of Mexican gangsters, all of them strapped – carrying loaded firearms.

The gang Joker took us to were called Cali's Finest and they weren't shy when it came to expressing themselves. As I stood there, they graffitied a huge concrete wall with their tag, and then one of them – a young gangster with brown skin and short hair – explained their philosophy. 'Fuck niggers, homey. Any nigger that passes by here, we'll fucking shoot those motherfuckers. *Kill* those motherfuckers. That's the 'hood right there. No one wants to fuck with this 'hood.'

I wondered if they ever had to be wary of writing their graffiti in this area. 'No, man,' he replied. 'We don't give a fuck. This is our 'hood. Anyone who steps in here and wants to fuck with us . . . this is ours right here. We roll everywhere we control, and we control everywhere we fucking roll. Anyone who fucking rolls down here, we'll blast those motherfuckers. This is *our* hood, homey. You don't want to fuck with our 'hood. Anyone who comes down here who's black, fucking blast those motherfuckers. Kill blacks. It's all about that brown, that's what's up.'

It was aggressive and mouthy. It might have just been bravado were it not for the fact that every one of these gang members was strapped. And the guy who was talking to me was little more than a kid. A friend of his, though, was an old man by gang standards: twenty-four years of age. His name was Pisto and he had done well to survive the streets for as long as he had. His face was all smashed up – he'd been beaten up by another gang recently, and although he managed to get away, it wasn't without some serious punishment. 'The thing that protects me,' he stated, 'is this.' From his jeans he pulled a Glock, and not a standard nine-millimetre either. This thing was a hand cannon, a weapon that's going to put a very big hole in whatever it gets fired at. It was fully loaded with forty-five rounds and Pisto was waving around like a toy. 'This is what protects me every day. I never leave it home.'

I asked Pisto what he thought of the other gangs around him.

'If they're not from where I'm from, fuck 'em. They ain't nothing. They're bitches. You know why? Because they'll shoot me as quick as I'll shoot them.'

I didn't doubt it.

Pisto was high. I don't know what on, but my instincts told me it was more than weed. He pulled his Glock out again. 'Look at my gun!' he insisted. 'It's loaded! I'm a gangster!'

I was getting tired of break-dancing around the end of Pisto's pistol and to avoid being shot we decided to leave. Pisto would have given us another interview, but a couple of days later he was arrested. I don't know what the charges were, but they were enough to get him put in the county jail. If we were going to find out more about the Mexicans, we would have to hope that Joker liked what he learned when he started asking around about us.

It seemed he did. Over the next few days I hung with him quite a lot. I needed to gain his trust before he would talk in front of the cameras, and that meant a lot of time just hanging out, smoking cigarettes and drinking. On one occasion, Joker, his crew and I went to buy some booze. Walking into a liquor store, we encountered a bunch of people from a rival gang. There's a mantra that gets repeated when these people meet: 'Where you from?' Sounds like an innocent question, but it's one you have to make sure you give the right answer to. You can't just say LA – they want to know which 'hood or which gang. And if you refuse to say? Well, then you're a pussy and you get shot. All the Hispanics went through the ritual and then they came to me. I was confidently assuming that they wouldn't take me for a south Los Angeles Latino gang member. But no. 'Where you from?'

I looked around a bit nervously. All eyes were on me and everyone was waiting to hear what I had to say.

'Er, London?' I ventured.

The rival gangsters looked at each other. Obviously London wasn't a 'hood they were familiar with. There was an uncomfortable silence from both sides.

And then the rival gang went on their way. I breathed a sigh of relief.

Looking back it was funny; at the time it was deadly serious. Joker told me I'd handled the situation well and I think it won me some credibility with him. Enough, anyway, for him to continue hanging with me, but not quite enough for me to be fully taken into his trust. Not yet.

One of Joker's crew was a self-styled skiptracer – someone who finds people who don't want to be found. Given the blood in, blood out nature of most gangs, you can well imagine that there are a number of people who fall into this category. Joker's skiptracer wanted me to be in no doubt that he was skilled at his job. He had a distinctive Mexican accent and while we were hanging out he sidled up to me on more than one occasion. 'I could find you, Ross Kemp,' he continuously told me. 'I could find you easily.'

He didn't say any more than that, but his implication was clear. If we turned these guys over, if we misrepresented them in any way, if we weren't quite who we said we were, the repercussions for us would be severe. Terminal, in fact. No matter how friendly I became with Joker, I never forgot that there was this underlying threat. I never forgot how important it was to treat these men with the proper respect. Diss some gangs and they'll just chase you off their block; diss these guys and they'll find you. Wherever you are.

Dissing someone, of course, can come in many forms. As part of Joker and I getting to know each other, the crew and I took his family out for Mexican food one Sunday lunchtime. Joker had a wife and three boys, so with them and the crew it was quite a big party. We had with us a researcher who came from a good Mexican family. There's a bit of snobbery going on between the Californian Mexicans and those who still live in Mexico, the Californians thinking that they've done better – they're a cut above – so our researcher was the subject of a bit of gentle ribbing. He was a very well-dressed man. At the end of each day, when the rest of us were covered in sweat and filth having been in all kinds of places, he was always still immaculate; and he looked immaculate at that Sunday lunch too, in a well-pressed shirt and smart trousers.

It was the shirt, I think, that caught the eye of Joker Junior, the middle of the three boys and what you would have to call a lively kid. Joker Junior kept eyeing the neatly pressed shirt and brandishing a spoonful of refried beans, waving it around and teasing the researcher with it. He chose his moment to flick the food as carefully as a sniper aiming at his target, and he had the pinpoint accuracy of a professional hitman. The refried beans splatted all over our researcher's face and shirt.

He looked understandably outraged and I sensed everybody holding their breath. Did this guy *really* want to reprimand Joker's son in front of his dad? To try and ease the tension, I smiled. It seemed to work. Joker burst out laughing. Of course, this only encouraged Joker Junior. The second and third splats of refried beans came in pretty quick succession.

The researcher stood up. He was really quite upset by now and he said something to the kid in Spanish.

That was the point when Joker stopped laughing.

Fortunately, the episode in the restaurant didn't jeopardize our relationship with him, and he eventually invited us and the cameras into his house.

Joker lived in Riverside, home to the University of California and birthplace of the Californian citrus industry. All in all not a bad part of town. It's not Beverley Hills, but it's not Compton either. The street in which he lived was well-to-do, a far better neighbourhood than any I had been in before during my investigation into the gangs of LA. Parked outside were two new cars, one of them an SUV. This was not the house of a poor person and Joker sure as hell didn't earn his crust working nine to five.

He opened the door to me holding a beer and wearing a vest that displayed his considerable bulk and his many Mayan tattoos. His whole skin was plastered with them. I asked him if he would explain to me the reason why he had covered himself with ink. It was, he told me, a cultural thing. 'When they used to sacrifice people, they used to kill them and peel off their skin, then put it on themselves. It means, you fuck with me, I'm going to put your skin on me. You're a dead motherfucker.'

Joker got his first tattoo in prison, more out of boredom than anything else. But as time passed, the tattoos started to become more significant. 'I started earning shit. I was whacking fools in the joint. Stabbing fools, or whatever.'

Under orders?

'Yeah, under orders, of course.'

And would that be people in Latino gangs?

'Any Latino that was disobeying, they had to get regulated, know what I mean? So we got to deal with them.'

Deal with them. Sounded ominous. I wondered exactly what it meant – to hurt or to kill.

'To hurt them. But sometimes to kill too. Motherfucker needs to get killed, he needs to get killed, regardless.'

Joker gave me a guided tour of his tattoos. Around his neck were the words, 'I'm just a soul whose intentions are good.'

'Because I am,' he told me. And something in his eyes made me think that he really believed that. As he said it, he glanced over at his family, who were in the room with us. I'm sure, somehow, that his intentions as far as they were concerned were for the best. But then I couldn't help remembering what it is that paves the way to hell . . .

Joker's most telling tattoos, however, were on his head. In order for us to see them, he had to go and shave. When he returned bald-headed, he grinned at me. 'Now I look like Ross Kemp!'

Inside prison, he explained, having a shaved head is part of the culture. But there's a practical reason for it too: if you don't have any hair, no one can grab it in the middle of a fight. Across the back of his head, written in big letters, was 'SURENO'. Self-explanatory, really. At the top of his forehead was, 'It wasn't me.' 'That's for the cops,' he told me. 'So if I get busted, it wasn't me.' Along the left of his head was a deep scar, accompanied by 'I'm still standing.' Joker explained that he had been hit with a barbell in prison. We're not talking about a dumbbell here, we're talking about an entire barbell. I don't know how much it weighed, but it was enough to crack his skull and put a dent in his head.

But despite the severity of the blow, 'I didn't fucking fall. I was still standing there.'

Sounded to me like he'd earned that one all right.

Finally we got to the piece of ink that I really wanted to know about. Just behind his left ear Joker had a picture of a man screaming. What happened there? I wondered. For the first time since I'd arrived, I saw him turn almost coy. 'Well, I can't tell you about that,' he tiptoed around the question. 'But it is what it is.'

I knew enough about prison gangs by now to realize that if you awarded yourself a stripe for something you hadn't done, chances are you'd end up being killed. So whatever it was Joker had done to earn that tattoo, it had made someone scream. A lot.

I tried to get him to elaborate, but the bar was quite obviously shut.

Silence. That was what I came up against when I started asking Joker questions he didn't want to answer. It didn't matter how much I courted him or how much he trusted me. He was abiding by some code of silence and he wasn't going to break it.

I'd learned a lot from him, however, not least that there was some kind of hierarchy among the Mexicans in prison. Receive an order to kill someone and you have to do it. It sounded to me like the prison-gang culture I had encountered during my time in Orange County and Pelican Bay was just as thriving among the Hispanics taking over parts of Los Angeles.

The information I gleaned from Joker was backed up by my police contacts. They told me that ultimate control of the Hispanic street gangs was held by one group: a prison gang called the Mexican Mafia, or La eMe. None of the

Mexicans I had met – not the boys from Cali's Finest, not even Joker – would talk about them. Quite clearly La eMe held a firm grip on its own power. And so to try and find out more about what was clearly a terrifying organization, I travelled to the north of LA, to Kern Valley State Prison, eight hours out of Los Angeles and home to 5,000 inmates. As I was informed by a prison guard with a certain amount of understatement, 'These people aren't necessarily in here for singing too loud in church.' I was told not to wear my regular filming outfit of jeans and black T-shirt. In Kern State only the prisoners wear jeans. If there's a riot or someone attacks another prisoner and the prison guards have to start shooting, you don't want to be wearing the same clothes as the inmates.

A and B wings of Kern State are in permanent lockdown because of the ongoing war there between the blacks and the Hispanics. I knew there was no hope that any prison members of La eMe would talk to me, but in Kern State there is a special wing – C – for inmates who have turned state's evidence. For them, that means only one thing: they've been green-lit. This means that whatever gang they used to be a member of have ordered a hit on them. Put them back in to the regular prison community and they'll die. No question. Let them back out on the streets and the future doesn't look much rosier. This is the end of the line, the place where gang members go when they've nowhere else to turn. Blacks, whites and Hispanics – even a few sex offenders – all mix in a way that you simply wouldn't see in other parts of the prison.

Despite the fact that there's really not much more that the Latinos in C Wing could do to upset La eMe, volunteers to talk to us were pretty thin on the ground. Only one was willing to give us the inside track. His name was Angel, and his story was a shocking one.

Angel was in his fifties, a bit shorter than me, well built (he had been pumping iron in the exercise yard for some thirty years) with a grey moustache and dark cropped hair going grey at the sides. He was a quiet man. Subdued even. Pass Angel in the street and you wouldn't notice him. They say that the eyes are the window to the soul. Well, if that's the case, I feared for Angel's spirit. The only thing that keeps him going nowadays, he told me, is playing basketball. We sat down together in a stark white room with nothing but a table, two chairs and big windows looking on to the corridor so people could see what was happening inside. Angel was, to say the least, reluctant to talk to us. But he did.

Angel grew up in a Hispanic area of LA called the San Gabriel Valley. He joined a Latino gang that went by the name of Sangra at the age of twelve. I asked him if he was forced to join the gang and he shook his head. 'I wanted it,' he told me. When he was thirteen he had his first taste of imprisonment – for assault with a deadly weapon. If a spell in juvenile hall was intended to deter him from the gangster lifestyle, however, it didn't. When he left he returned immediately to the bosom of the gang where, in his words, 'We just broke the law, partied, did what we wanted to do.'

Angel was still only thirteen when he started hitting connection houses – places where drug dealers operate from. It's a common way for gang members to get money. Roll a regular member of the public and the police will get called out. Your fingerprints might get found; certainly there's a chance you're going to get caught. But roll a drug dealer and what's he going to do – walk into the local cop shop and complain that some punks stole his stash? It's the reason a lot of drug dealers carry guns. What was different about Angel's connection-house hits, however, was that he carried them out with his dad, who was a heroin addict. Angel was used because he was a kid who no one would pay any attention to. 'I used to make the first move on somebody. Stab them while they took all the stuff, and then they would take them out. Kill them. That's how I was getting money.'

He was in the eighth grade when all this was happening, so he was familiar with violence from a very early age. The thirteen-year-old Angel really didn't stand a chance.

As time passed, Angel began to find life in the Sangra gang boring. There were no leaders as such, no real hierarchy. Nowhere to go. And so he branched out, making contact with other gangs. If he got along with them, they would party together and Angel would bring them into his neighbourhood. If they didn't get along, he'd go into their territory shooting. Teenage kicks, only with guns.

It was in the county jail at the age of twenty-one that Angel was approached by a Mexican Mafia member who would later become his *padrino* – his godfather, the man who would ultimately sponsor him for membership of La eMe. His *padrino* had a court case coming up and someone in the jail was going to testify against him. Angel attacked the grass with a knife. He didn't kill him – the victim ran off screaming – but he did enough damage for his loyalty to La eMe to be clear. When he and his *padrino* left jail, they started running together. And killing together. It was with this man that Angel was arrested for murder. His *padrino* got the death sentence, Angel got life without parole. He's still serving that sentence today.

It's not the only sentence he's serving, however. The killing didn't stop just because Angel was in prison. Now a fully signed-up member of La eMe, it fell to him to carry out a hit on another member. It happened in Folsom State Prison. 'He broke a rule of ours,' Angel explained, 'which states that you can't put your hand on another brother –

fighting, none of that stuff. This guy did, so they threw a vote that said he has to go. And since he was my neighbour, I went into his cell and did it.'

But surely, I asked him, he knew what would happen if he got caught.

Angel shrugged. 'We have rules,' he said flatly. He was awarded another life sentence for the hit.

He ended up in Pelican Bay. But as time passed Angel gradually became more and more disillusioned with the way La eMe was being run. And so, after twenty-seven years of being a member, he decided to leave. La eMe, however, is not just something you walk out of. Angel turned state's evidence and was transferred to C Wing of Kern State. As I was talking to him, I couldn't help but feel a sense of jaded regret. 'Twenty-seven years in La eMe, and then one day just to say, "I'm gone." It's hard. I didn't want to leave. I still have friends. There are still members up there that I like. But I know that if we were able to get at each other, it would be on, we'd go at each other. I'm not a fool.'

Does it bother Angel, being green-lit? Apparently not. 'They have to come this way to get me. And that would mean they have to check in. You don't check in just to go after somebody, unless they send a sleeper. They'd have to give up information to come on this side, and I'm not that important.' I hoped he was right, but the truth was that I don't think he really cared that much. Not any more.

Angel's perspective on La eMe was interesting because, in gang terms, he was a really old guy. He'd seen it all and he was able to explain to me how times had changed. When he was a member of an LA street gang, any money that came into his hands by illegal means was his to spend. Nowadays, however, the Mexican Mafia have such a strong hold over the street gangs from their prison cells that a proportion of any money 'earned' on the street has to be paid directly to them.

So you're a member of the Mexican Mafia. You're serving 300 years in the SHU at Pelican Bay. What good is all this money to you? 'Well,' Angel told me, 'they give the money to their wives and kids so that they can buy houses and cars. That's about it, because they can't use it in the canteen! It's for status – they go around bragging about how much they have.'

Angel may have become disillusioned with the way La eMe was going, but he had given me a lot of invaluable information about the way the organization worked. He must have given the authorities a good deal more, because you don't get yourself a pass to C Wing of Kern State for nothing. You have to give up hard facts. And from what I was learning about La eMe, that was a dangerous thing to do.

Lieutenant John Gaza of Kern State's gang investigation unit agreed to meet and tell me more. He had spent a good deal of time trying to understand La eMe, and he knew a lot about how they worked. I asked him how people managed to get information in and out of prison, how La eMe's instructions are handed down to the street gangs and to other members in other prisons. He explained to me that written messages were keestered, just as I had learned in Pelican Bay. What I hadn't seen in the Bay, however, were the actual messages that the Mexicans wrote. Not wanting, for obvious reasons, to insert reams of A4 into their rectal cavities, one of the first things that members of La eMe are taught to do is to write small. And I mean *really* small. I was shown some examples. Hundreds of words, thousands even, are squeezed onto a piece of paper the size of your palm. This is rolled up and inserted where the sun doesn't shine. The screws are wise to this method of transporting information, of course, but you can't put your finger in every arsehole, even if you're inclined to. Of course, if you *do* manage to intercept one of these incredibly skilfully written messages, you can glean a lot of information about what's going on inside the cells.

What was still not clear to me, however, was why gangs on the streets would take orders from prison inmates serving life sentences. Lieutenant Gaza explained. 'The Mexican Mafia controls the prisons, and basically they tell the street gang members, if you do not do our bidding, eventually you're going to come to the jail, or your family is, and we will go ahead and deal with them then. Or we'll deal with you then.' If you're a gangster, chances are you *will* do time at some stage. And when that time comes, it pays to be on the right side of the people in charge. This is especially true when the people in charge are La eMe, as I was about to find out.

Lieutenant Gaza laid out some photos in front of me. They were truly sickening. There were a few examples of soft hits — warning shots to people who had stepped out of line in prison: bloodied faces, cut-up skin, often from illegal weapons not unlike the ones I'd seen in Pelican Bay. A 'tomahawk', for example, is a weapon made by melting a razor blade into the handle of a plastic toothbrush and then strapping it in place with twine so it doesn't come out in the victim's body. These tomahawks can also be used to inflict what Lieutenant Gaza referred to as a hard hit. And trust me, you don't want one of these. This is a way of singling someone out as a grass. It's a deep, long gash called a *puto* mark – *puto* being Spanish for faggot or homosexual. The *puto* mark is inflicted on the face if possible, but often elsewhere. I was shown one picture of a victim's back. It looked like a butchered piece of meat, with huge valleys of cut-open flesh – wounds that looked to me like they would never heal.

If you know that one day you'll be spending time inside, I think you'd do pretty much anything to make sure you didn't end up like that.

The power that La eMe wielded over the Hispanic street gangs of LA was starting to be revealed to me. And when I compared this control to the sprawling mass of Bloods and Crips on the streets of Compton, it was clear why the Mexicans, who seemed more organized, more ruthless and more downright scary, appeared to be winning the power struggle with the blacks. They had a command centre and a structure. They had discipline and rules that were brutally enforced. Most of all, people were very, very scared of them.

The fact that so few people were willing to speak to me about La eMe was testament to the culture of fear that they had engendered. There was, however, one more person who was prepared to talk. He used to run with La eMe, but now he held a grudge against them as a result of a drug deal that had gone wrong. He was a marked man. He was green-lit. He covered his face when the cameras were on and his identity was never revealed to us. This was an understandably paranoid man. The meeting took place at a secret location off Sunset Strip – a motel that looked like something straight out of a Quentin Tarantino movie, where the carpets couldn't have been stickier if you'd covered them in Copydex. Inside the motel room the toilet had a plastic seal on it stating that it had been recently cleaned, but you could still see flecks of shit down the side of the bowl, so God only knows when it had last seen the business end of a toilet brush. There were cigarette burns all up the wall, and sitting on the bed was like parking your arse on Jell-O – clearly it had received some pretty punishing use. How anyone could

162

get turned on making out in a place like this I just don't know, but from the stains on the duvet I reckoned plenty of people had.

My contact had been released from prison two years ago. I asked him about the beef between him and La eMe. 'They accused me of stealing money from them,' he said, 'so they put a green light on me. I was shot at, I got stabbed. Finally I just got tired of being stabbed so I stepped away from it.'

He described to me a paramilitary hierarchy, a top-down pyramid. The head of La eMe will have four generals. Each general will have four lieutenants, who'll have four sergeants and so on. 'In the streets,' he explained, 'every neighbourhood's going to have a soldier.' These soldiers are not actual members of La eMe – or 'brothers', as they are referred to – but 'associates'. 'An associate is a person who's trying to move in to being a brother. He's going to do a brother's dirty work.'

Will he kill for them?

'He'll kill for them. He'll rob for them. When I did it, I was told I could take a third of whatever I raked in. If it was $100,000, I took a third of that, and I gave the rest to them.'

And if he hadn't done that, what would have happened?

'Probably would have got killed.'

People on the street are so scared that dealers just hand over their dope and their dosh if they're approached by anyone claiming to be a brother. And no one goes around pretending, because woe betide anyone who does that. But what shocked me most about what I learned that day was that La eMe seemed to have no qualms about who they ordered to be killed. This man clearly bore a grudge against the Mexican Mafia. One allegation he made, which we have no evidence to substantiate, was that they are prepared to kill entire families in order to remove one of their enemies.

Inside prison, my contact told me, every young Hispanic gangster wants to be made because they know that when they finally leave prison – be it in five months or five years – they're going to have authority. And with that authority come all the things that every gangster wants: money, guns, dope and women.

'And when you're living in these neighbourhoods that we call the ghetto,' he told me simply, 'that's what we strive for.'

Before I left LA I had one more surprise in store. It came about as a result of a call from my new tattooed friend Joker, and he wasn't calling to say how much he was going to miss us. He was inviting us to a 'jump-in' – an initiation ceremony. A young man was going to be 'baptized' into a gang by being beaten up by four other members. The kid was only thirteen years old and was a cousin of Joker's. It sounds shocking, but in truth it's a rite of passage for many young men, not only those in the Latino gangs. And once he's jumped in, he's a gang member for life.

He was understandably nervous before the ceremony, but at no stage did I get the impression that he was doing this under duress. He wanted it. He was looking forward to it. Once in, he'd be part of a community. He'd have protection, people who would fight for him in this dangerous corner of America. He'd have the things they strive for in the ghetto, as my contact in the motel had put it. But as I looked at him, I couldn't help but remember Angel. I couldn't help but remember the dead look in his eyes as he spoke of a life wasted. I wondered what this kid, so eager to *be* someone, would think about gang membership when he reached Angel's age. *If* he reached Angel's age.

The kid might have been Joker's cousin, but that didn't

mean he got special treatment. The gang gave him a proper pasting as Joker counted – slowly – to thirteen. But he kept standing and by the end of it, his nose bloodied and his body bruised, I could sense the pride emanating from him. He wandered off with his new gangster buddies for a smoke and beer. It was a big night for that young teenager. A night to remember. In the grand scheme of things, however, he was just another statistic. It is estimated that in the last five years more than 20,000 young men have been jumped into Latino gangs.

Any organization with that kind of membership is a force to be reckoned with.

Prison gangs are a fact of life in Los Angeles. When I first went there to investigate the skinhead gangs of Orange County, I discovered that there was a subculture of highly ingenious gangsters in the SHU at Pelican Bay with a lot of time on their hands, and that the control they wielded on the streets was quite astonishing given the fact that most are incarcerated for the rest of their lives. But the Mexicans have taken this to a whole new level. It would appear that Hispanic gangs are the new dominant force on the streets of LA and their movements and activities are controlled by a brutally effective prison gang.

They demand respect and they get it; they demand silence and they get it. Of all the organizations I have encountered so far, La eMe are the most organized and feared. And for as long as they maintain this firm grip on power, the Latino gangs of LA will continue to thrive.

5. Kenya

Picture the scene. It's a slum on the outskirts of Nairobi. In a small hut made from corrugated zinc a mother is surrounded by four children. She is not in the rudest health, and nor are her kids. They are all hungry. Their surroundings are poor and none too clean. The grinding poverty they have to endure would turn the stomach of all but the most hardened. But still the children are boisterous, as children will be.

It's getting late. The kids are becoming more fractious. The mother wants to quieten them down, to make them go to sleep. In another part of the world she might whisper words into their little ears about the bogeyman or some other fiction invented to strike a little harmless fear into the minds of naughty children. But Africa holds enough terrors without having to worry about imaginary ones. Death and disease are commonplace. The children have seen it all. It's a daily part of their life.

And so the mother resorts to the one threat that she knows will make their tiny hearts skip a beat; she invokes the one name that strikes fear into huge swathes of the Kenyan population, be they children or grown-ups. 'Be good,' she tells them, her voice serious. 'Be good, or the Mungiki man will come and get you . . .'

This is no made-up scenario. From the slums of Nairobi to the tourist beaches of Mombasa, Kenyan children are urged to behave using that very threat. And being got by the Mungiki, I was told before I arrived in Nairobi, is not something you want to happen. They have a nasty little reputation for cutting off people's heads, arms and other parts of their anatomy. All in all, they make the Sandman sound like a pussycat.

The Mungiki, I was sure, would not take too kindly to being called a gang. They believe they have a higher calling than that. A divine calling, and a political mission. And yet the stories I had heard about them were grisly to say the least. Stories of protection rackets, extortion and extremely violent murder – the stock-in-trade of gangs around the world. Stories of a gang that strikes fear into the heart of the Kenyan population and that the government will go to almost any lengths to stamp out.

Before I flew to Kenya, I had no idea how close we would be able to get to the Mungiki; from the stories I had heard, I wasn't sure how close I *wanted* to get. What I didn't expect, however, was that we would arrive in this stricken country at one of the most turbulent times the gang had ever faced; I didn't expect to be admitted into the heart of a secretive sect, to be shown things that no camera had ever been allowed to film; and I didn't expect people I was there to investigate to end up dead before it was time for us to go home.

But Africa is like that. Violent. Volatile. Unpredictable. What I was to discover during my time in this troubled continent would shock me almost more than anything I had ever seen. Like Africa itself, my stay there was full of surprises and full of contrasts; it was thought-provoking and astonishing in equal measure; it made me realize, as a white man in the gritty backwaters of black Africa, that things are rarely either black or white. They are usually shades of grey.

*

167

To begin to understand the origins and rise of the Mungiki, you have to understand a little about the tribal nature of Kenyan society.

Our fixer was a man by the name of Tom, and he told me that as soon as he was old enough to understand what was being said to him, his father had sat him down and told him the history of their tribe – just as had been done to his father and his father's father. It was explained to Tom where the tribe had lived and where they had moved; it was explained to him who had done what to them, and when. Old enmities were reiterated, old allegiances reinforced. A sense of pride in his tribe was instilled into him. He explained to me that in Kenya your allegiance to the tribe comes before your allegiance to the country. It is everything.

There are at least forty-three different tribes in Kenya. Of these, the predominant tribe is that of the Kikuyu. In 1963 Kenya gained independence from the British empire. The end of colonial rule was due in part to the Mau Mau uprising. The Mau Mau were a vicious gang of rebels, largely from the Kikuyu tribe, who, it is often argued, forced the British from Kenya as a result of their horrific tactics. It should be pointed out that the British were a brutal occupying presence, but the Mau Mau's atrocities were considerable. Perhaps the most famous was the murder of a six-year-old white child hacked to death in his own bedroom. Pictures of the murdered child, along with his bloodstained teddy bears and toy trains, appeared in the Kenyan newspapers. In the end the colonialists decided they hadn't the stomach for such things, and left.

With the arrival of independence, it was a member of the Kikuyu tribe, Jomo Kenyatta, who became first prime minister and then president of Kenya. His vice-president was Daniel arap Moi, a member of the Kalenjin tribe. When

Kenyatta died in 1978, arap Moi became president. He retired in 2002 when he was constitutionally barred from running for a third term. He is now said to be one of the richest men in Africa. On his retirement he announced that his successor should be Jomo Kenyatta's son; Kenyatta Junior, however, was defeated in the presidential election by Mwai Kibaki, another Kikuyu. The next presidential election was held in December 2007. Kibaki was again inaugurated as president despite it being reasonably clear that his rival, Raila Odinga, had in fact won the election.

The Kenyan government, quite clearly, is no stranger to corruption. It is largely under the influence of the Kikuyu elite, a ruling group consisting of a few rich families that controls the trade – and therefore the money – within the country. This Kikuyu elite is a class apart from the poorer members of the tribe, but that doesn't mean that Kikuyus on the street are immune from the enmity of other tribes.

You don't have to be in Kenya very long to realize that government corruption is a fact of life. And, as is always the case when corruption rears its head at the highest level, the losers are invariably the people at the bottom. In the West, Kenya might have an image as the place to head to for high-end safaris or beach holidays with guaranteed sun, and it's true that such a side to the country certainly exists. What is beyond question, however, is that Nairobi has some of the most desperate slums I have ever seen. Three-quarters of the urban population live in these sprawling ghettos, and more than half of them have to survive on less than a dollar a day. There are slums, and then there are slums. There are areas of Nairobi that you can fly over and smell the stench of human excrement from the air. Dead rats lie in the street. By the time we had finished filming in Kenya, I had to throw my trainers away because they had rotted from contact with so much fecal matter. It is no surprise that gang clashes are rife, that violence thrives. And it is in places like this that the Mungiki have their power base.

My first port of call when we arrived was Mathari, a slum off the Thika Road on the outskirts of the capital. It's home to more than half a million people and is divided along tribal lines. Land is the most important thing to the Kenyan elite, and Mathari is built on land that nobody else wants – that's why the poor are allowed to live there. But there's no doubt that if that land were ever worth something, the poor would be wiped away from the area in an instant.

Like most slums, Mathari is built on slopes. Here, the slopes are covered in plastic bags and human waste – this is a place with no sanitation, a dumping ground that also happens to house humans. Mathari looks like it has been constructed exclusively from corrugated iron. Rivulets of cooking water and human urine drip down the streets into the river below. The further downhill you go, the worse the smell becomes, and it's not made any better by the overwhelming heat. Unemployment in Mathari is universal – there are no jobs, so the only way for people to get money is to go out of the slums and steal it, or to steal from each other.

Despite the level of poverty, the place seemed alive. Buzzing, almost. It's hot, busy and crowded. Music blares – a mixture of African rock, Baptist chants and tribal singing. The inhabitants of Mathari had nothing, but so many of them still seemed to have smiles on their faces. For people who were literally living in their own shit, they seemed happier than they deserved to be. Maybe their smiles were hiding something else. I don't know.

I was here to interview a young Kenyan called Sammy. Sammy had been to an English university and was prepared to explain to me, at great risk to himself, who the Mungiki were and how they operate. It was, I quickly found out, a brave thing for him to do. He was an earnest, well-spoken young man, and I was soon to understand why he was so worried about speaking out on camera.

'When the Mungiki first came into Mathari,' Sammy explained, 'they served a notice to anyone who was involved in crime, and they said, "We are the people who are now protecting the community. If you are caught stealing or doing anything, you will face us."'

I wondered what they had done to people who ignored their warning.

'One morning people woke up and there were four heads on that stretch over there.' He pointed towards a nearby hill. 'It was a very strong statement that they meant business. So just in a span of about a week there was no crime. This place was paradise again because the Mungiki policed it. Even the community appreciated the fact that they were here.'

The image Sammy was painting for me was one of a band of vigilantes dealing with the crime in the slums – a problem that the government clearly had no interest in – and being welcomed by the people. But things did not quite continue like that.

'Afterwards they resorted to asking people for money for protection. If you had a house within the area that they were claiming to protect, you were forced to pay thirty shillings.'

This sounded to me like nothing less than extortion. Moreover, it was extortion from people who were extremely poor. The Mungiki, it is claimed, manage to extract money from poor Kenyans in a variety of other ways, including taking payments from owners of *matatus* – vans that act as communal taxis – in return for protection. But the *matatu* owners don't have a choice in the matter. They either pay

171

to avoid violent attacks, or they suffer punishment from the Mungiki. All of a sudden, the organization's vigilantism had a different sheen to it. Sammy agreed. 'They would beat you up,' he said, 'just to make you understand you have to pay. There's no way out of it.'

Sammy's opinion of the Mungiki was pretty plain, but he did admit that they had brought some benefits to the slums. 'They brought electricity,' he told me. 'They were the only people who had the nerve to steal electricity from the Kenya Power and Lighting Company and then supply it down here. But you had to pay for it.' The price they charged for their stolen electricity was 300 shillings per light bulb per month. That works out at around $4.50 – a considerable sum in Mathari.

As Sammy spoke, he led me over a bridge which crossed a wide stream. The smell here was almost intolerable: the banks of the stream were literally covered with rubbish bags, and there was human shit running down the sides and into the water. As we stood there, a little boy approached the edge of the bridge. He pulled down his trousers and ejected an explosive spray of diarrhoea into the water. He wiped himself with his hand and then went on his way. Nobody around me batted an eyelid.

I tried to put my mind back on the job in hand and asked Sammy what happened if you crossed the Mungiki, if you refused to do what they demanded. 'They would abduct you,' Sammy told me, his voice becoming more intense. 'One of the people who was abducted – I don't know how he crossed them but his head ended up there.' He pointed towards an area of the rubbish-strewn riverbank. 'His legs –' now Sammy pointed further along '– were not very far away. His upper body was found where Mathari ends.' So his torso was found a mile away from where his head and his legs ended up. A grisly business, but even more grisly when you consider the symbolism behind such actions. Many Kenyans believe that if your body is not buried whole then your soul cannot pass into the afterlife. The dismemberment for which the Mungiki were notorious was more than just a corporeal punishment; it was a spiritual one as well.

'When this started happening,' Sammy continued, 'even the community started asking themselves questions.'

I bet they did.

Abductions, dismembered bodies – what Sammy was describing to me was truly the stuff of nightmares. It was hard to imagine what was in the mind of someone prepared to cut another human being up – possibly while they were still alive – then carry their head, arms and legs a mile so that they can be scattered around. No wonder little Kenyan children were forced into good behaviour by threats of the Mungiki man. But at face value, Sammy explained to me, there was nothing nightmarish about them. 'They look like decent people. They don't drink, they don't smoke, they just take snuff. It's tricky. They come with a face that says, "We care. We are providing a service." But it takes time before you start seeing the ugliness.'

It might take time, but it seemed to me that when the ugliness started showing itself, it was the sort of thing that was likely to stay with you for ever. And despite what Sammy was telling me, the Mungiki had supporters. A lot of them. Millions, in fact. Clearly there was more to this than met the eye.

The Mungiki have been outlawed by the government. As such, they are targeted by the Kenyan police. As with everything surrounding the Mungiki, however, their relationship with the police is not as straightforward as it might appear. In Kenya the police are a feared organization themselves.

Many Kenyans see the police force as little more than the strong arm of a corrupt government. They are not there to protect the people; they are there to protect those in power. And, like so many in authority in Kenya, the police are not untainted by the corruption that seems so endemic in the country.

Kenya has a big problem with illegal alcohol, perhaps the most widespread example of which is *changaa*, a drink distilled from a variety of grains, maize being the most common. It's incredibly potent and often dangerous – *changaa* is the cause of a large number of deaths in Kenya every year. Its toxicity is not only down to its high alcohol content. A lot of *changaa* is made from river water, and, as I'd already seen, Kenyan river water is a long way from being the purest Highland spring. You know when you see someone on *changaa*: they're absolutely out of their head. And if you're a *changaa* addict, you don't care where it's from; you just care that you've got some.

Despite *changaa* being illegal, production is widespread. Traditionally the police have turned a blind eye to it in return for bribes. The Mungiki, however, saw a business opportunity and muscled in on the deal, demanding a 'tax' from the producers of the drink in the areas that they controlled. The police, of course, did not take kindly to such interference, and in May 2007 tensions came to a head in Mathari when two policeman were shot dead and their weapons stolen. The police came in to exact their revenge. They despatched the GSU – the General Service Unit – a paramilitary wing of the police consisting of highly trained officers. When Sammy mentioned the GSU to me, he seemed to bristle. 'Oh boy,' he said. 'You don't want them.'

He explained to me what the GSU did when they entered Mathari. 'The shooting started. The beating. Everybody was asked to come out of their houses. If you were caught inside then they would beat you or shoot you. In a span of six hours, thirty-five people had been killed. They were here to make a statement, and when you make a statement, you make it to the fullest. They raped women.'

I was shocked by what I was being told. Police raping women? In the same area where I was standing right now? Sammy nodded. 'There is what goes on record, and what doesn't go on record,' he told me. 'It was horrific what happened.'

That sounded to me like an understatement. Later in my stay I had an opportunity to put this accusation to a police representative. He told me that it wasn't true, and that on the occasion Sammy was talking about the press were there all the time. It was a somewhat hollow denial, especially given that the press in Kenya is largely state-controlled.

The Mungiki sounded vicious enough. But it was beginning to become clear to me that it was not just them who had blood on their hands.

The police and the Mungiki. From what I had heard so far, there didn't seem to be much to choose between them. I couldn't quite work out who the bad guys were in this scenario. Maybe they were both bad guys, and the ordinary, impoverished citizens of Kenya were being caught in their crossfire. Whatever the truth, the following day I was given the opportunity to see at first hand something of the enmity that existed between the two groups.

Over the past few months there had been rumours that hundreds of Mungiki sympathizers had been rounded up by the police and never seen again. Tensions were boiling over just as we arrived in Nairobi and that morning word came through to us that things were coming to a head. The previous day in a slum called Kayole an angry mob had laid siege to a police station holding a Mungiki suspect. The police were forced to release the suspect, but there was no way that was going to be the end of the matter. That morning hundreds of police had arrived in Kayole to begin the reprisals and, thanks to our brilliant fixer Tom, we were the first to know about it. We arrived in Kayole just as the police vans were storming in, searching for Mungiki.

It was obvious from the moment we got there that the arrival of the police was not something that the local population took lightly. The streets were almost deserted. On our way in, we passed a line of Kenyans lying prostrate on the floor. They didn't move a muscle and at first I thought they were dead. They had been told to lie still, and they knew that if they so much as twitched, they'd have a bullet in them courtesy of the aggressive-looking police officer watching over them. You get an itch, you'd better not scratch it.

The further we drove into Kayole, the more I realized that we were putting ourselves into the middle of an extremely dangerous situation. Almost all the inhabitants had climbed up on to balconies or onto the roofs – no one wanted to be on the streets, because on the streets you were likely to get shot. But the streets were where we as a crew had to be. I'd been on raids before, and the team was well used to putting itself in harm's way. But of all the things we'd ever done, this was one of the most foolhardy. We were on nobody's side: the police wouldn't protect us, the Mungiki wouldn't protect us. It was as tense as any situation we'd put ourselves in – and I include my time in Afghanistan in that.

As we left the vehicle and made our way up the main street, I saw what looked like a few civilians carrying AK-47s. At first I assumed that these were Mungiki, but it was then explained to me that in fact they were more likely to be plainclothes police. Any Mungiki, by now, had cleared well away. I wanted to talk to a member of the police, but none of them would speak to me. Eventually I approached a police car with its attendant officer. He looked like Idi Amin, and acted like him. He demanded to know who I was, so I told him that I was from Sky TV, England. The response I got was far from welcoming. 'You go home,' I was instructed. 'This is our internal problem here. You go home.' It was clearly all the interview I was going to get.

'I'm not going home,' I muttered, visibly scared.

In the distance we heard gunfire, and with it came the sound of screaming. We started walking towards the noise. The crowds of Kenyans on the balconies and roofs called down at us not to head that way, and anyone left on the street certainly seemed to be going in the opposite direction. Before long, we saw groups of people being rounded up and loaded on to open-top police trucks. They were forced to lie down flat and were driven away. I didn't know if they were protesters or not, but I did know I was glad it wasn't me being driven off by the Kenyan police.

There were rocks being thrown, and suddenly there was more gunfire and bursts of tear gas. People on the street dispersed like a flock of birds. Down a side street we saw a young man being arrested. He was beaten sharply round the head. 'Just kill me,' he called as he passed us. 'Just kill me.'

He too was loaded on to a truck.

Joining him was another young man. He had short dreadlocks and this, I knew, was a sign of Mungiki member-ship – a bit like tattoos in other gangs – though many of them have got rid of their dreads in order to escape detection at times like these. He too was roughly manhandled into the truck and then driven away.

What I witnessed that day was a police force striking fear into the heart of a population and using brutal and heavy-handed techniques to assert their authority. No doubt they were ostensibly there to round up Mungiki sympathizers, but it all looked pretty random to me. Sammy had told me that the police had raided Mathari the previous year to make a statement. Well, they were making a statement here too. They were telling the whole community of Kayole what they could expect if they supported and harboured the Mungiki. The message was delivered loud and clear: you could almost taste the fear emanating from the civilian population. I was left in no doubt that day that no matter how bad the Mungiki were, the Kenyan police and GSU were a terrifying force. They were people you didn't want to cross. I was beginning to think that the biggest gang in Kenya was not the Mungiki, but the government and the police.

When we first arrived in Kenya we didn't know how much access we were going to get to the Mungiki. They're a secret organization, they're illegal, and in a country where television cameras are viewed with suspicion, there was a good chance that they were going to be pretty camera-shy. Our best hope was that we would get to speak to the Mungiki street gangs, the foot soldiers of the organization. The day after the riot in Kayole, however, we received a call. Certain strands of the Mungiki leadership had clearly noted our presence and we were offered an audience with three top members. The rendezvous point was some way from the relative safety of central Nairobi, and after everything we had heard about these people we approached the meet with a certain amount of trepidation.

There is a mythology surrounding the Mungiki, and much of that mythology centres around the life of their leader,

Maina Njenga. Our destination that day was Njenga's house, deep in the heartland of Mungiki territory.

Njenga is a fascinating character – at least, the history he has constructed for himself is. He was born in the country's mountain regions – often called the White Highlands because after the Second World War only the European inhabitants of Kenya were allowed to lease farms there. It is said that he was always a strange boy when he was growing up, claiming to have had visions and the like, but nobody believed him. The story goes that one day he fell very ill and died. He came back to life, then went off into the wilderness. When he returned, he had received a vision for his people, the Kikuyu. He devised a pseudo-religion, with himself as the figurehead, into which young Kenyans might be baptized and which would offer hope to people who have none. Fanciful stuff, of course, and when I was told these stories of reincarnation, spells in the wilderness and baptism, it was pretty obvious to me that someone had been reading a book bigger than any I'll ever write.

As a result of his visions, Maina Njenga formed the Mungiki, or 'multitude'. The name is apt. Before long the Mungiki had grown from being one man to many. He spoke to the poor, disaffected Kikuyus; he held anti-government rallies. Former members of the Mau Mau joined, telling the young Mungiki that the modern country was no different to colonial Kenya. The Mungiki became a substantial political force, but they were outlawed by the government and so aligned themselves with a political party called the Kenya National Youth Alliance to give themselves a political voice, albeit an unofficial one.

Maina Njenga is currently serving a five-year prison sentence. It is said that drugs and a gun were found in his house. It is also alleged that the gun was without a firing

179

pin, making it as much use as a cat flap in an elephant house. Whether Njenga takes drugs or not I couldn't say, but I remembered Sammy telling me that the Mungiki were a clean-living lot. Certainly Njenga has always claimed that his movement is a peaceful one. And maybe he was right. Maybe the atrocities carried out in Mathari and elsewhere were the actions of out-of-control street gangs, kids claiming to be Mungiki but very far removed from the movement's origins and power base. I was beginning to suspect that there was more to the Mungiki than met the eye, and I determined to approach the meeting with their leadership with an open mind.

Njenga's home was deserted. There was no security around it, which somehow added to the sense of history that seemed to shine from the place: there were no guards because nobody would dare go near the house. Our contacts were yet to arrive, so we let ourselves in. The house had clearly been emptied when the Mungiki leader was imprisoned, and there was something unspeakably eerie about it as we stood inside and waited. On one wall of the main room there was a weird mosaic filled with all kinds of disparate religious symbolism. There were biblical crosses, Arab crescent moons, tribal scrawls – it looked like a monument to the hotchpotch religion Njenga had created. His house had the atmosphere of a shrine, but a shrine to what, I wasn't quite sure. Certainly I didn't get a cathedral-like sense of peace in this place. Across my back I have a scar. Whenever I'm nervous, whenever I find myself in a tense situation, the scar starts to itch. Believe me, it was itching like anything as I waited for the Mungiki to turn up.

Eventually we heard people arrive. There were three men, along with their wives and a fourth woman. I didn't realize it at the time, but this was Maina Njenga's wife, Virginia. I

Dandora, Nairobi's principal landfill site

The Mungiki are accused of performing horrific acts of violence

The police arrive in a slum called Kayole, searching for Mungiki

The air was filled with angry shouts and thick black smoke from burning tyres

An angry Mungiki mob take to the streets after the murder of Maina Njenga's wife

Talking to Charles Ndungu, the acting leader of the Mungiki political organization

Before a meeting with the government, Charles's car was ambushed and a shower of bullets rained down upon him. Charles died instantly

With a group of gang members from Norris Green in Liverpool

The Noggses show me the weapons they use in their ongoing war with the Croccy Crew

A selection of guns confiscated from the Croccy Crew and the Noggses by the Matrix

would find out later in my stay that this was a dangerous position to hold. It was the men, however, who were here to talk to me today. Their names were Steven Njenga, Charles Ndungu and Joe Waiganjo. They were calm, confident individuals, well-spoken and intelligent. They wore suits and shirts – fashionable clobber for Kenyan young men. I remembered the state of the people I had seen in Mathari, and I wondered where the trio in front of me found the money to buy such clothes.

I would also find out later that Charles was the acting leader of the organization while Maina Njenga was in prison. But it was Joe who did most of the talking. He was a smooth-talking dude, with sharp lapels and a slightly louche manner. Joe was the head of the Mungiki political wing and was known among them as 'the General'. I asked them why the government wanted Maina Njenga in jail. Joe barely missed a beat before responding. 'They fear our might,' he said. 'The numbers, the people who are our members.'

And did they know how many members they had?

'Three million,' Steven told me. That's quite a gang.

I wanted to ask the three of them about some of the unpleasant stories I had heard about the Mungiki. I didn't know what their reaction would be, but I went ahead anyway. What of the accusation, I asked, that if you try to leave the Mungiki, you get killed.

'That's a good lie,' Joe told me with a perfectly straight face. 'That's a very big lie. This negative propaganda against us started back in 1997. Before that, there was not a lot of negative propaganda. They were at least giving the stories as they are. But after they saw the growth of the movement . . . that is when the propaganda came out of a negative nature.'

There are degrees, of course, of negative propaganda, and not all of what I knew about the Mungiki came from government sources. I asked Joe about the rumours that they cut people's heads off, that they dismember bodies and leave the parts in different places.

'They are all very good fabrications from the state machinery. The fear that the government have propagated has worked, but it's not us that do anything.'

The Mungiki leadership denied all accusations of violence, but they didn't deny the fact that they run the slums in certain areas of Nairobi. How did they do that? How did they operate?

Steven answered my question – sort of. 'In the slum areas,' he told me, 'people are desperate. They have no hope. We went in there and started organizing them.'

But there must have been gangs inside the slums who weren't happy about the Mungiki turning up. Presumably they weren't just handed a cup of milky tea and told to settle down. The three of them laughed. 'We changed those rude boys,' he told me. 'We give them reality and hope.'

But these rude boys, as he called them, are street kids who only understand violence. Truthfully, how could you change such a person?

'First,' Joe explained, 'you have to change his mental perspective to life. He should not just be violent, he should think about his future.'

So, no head-chopping then. At least, not according to the well-dressed Mungiki in front of me. I wondered if the trio would admit to me that they levy taxes on the people inside the slums.

'We assist one another,' Joe told me instantly. 'We don't levy taxes. They all know that we have a common problem. The poverty is common. So they need something like a welfare system that the government did not create for them, so the people create it for themselves. We help them with the organization. Let the people contribute a shilling, five shillings, ten shillings, twenty.'

And are these contributions entirely voluntary? If I didn't want to give five shillings, what would happen?

Steven took over. 'It would depend,' he said. 'What normally happens is, during times like campaign periods, that is when there is need for money.' He hadn't said that contributions *weren't* voluntary, but he hadn't denied it either.

Joe continued. 'Kenya is not yet free,' he told me. 'What we are going through is colonization by the black elite. They own at least 65 per cent of the land mass in Kenya. Until that is addressed, Kenya will never be free.'

And this minority that controls the majority – are they the ones that have it in for the Mungiki? It seemed to be the case. The three told me that their main problem was not with the government, but with the handful of very powerful people who are able to control the government's policies. 'They are able to control the investments that the government is going to undertake. They are able to control the money flow. That's why they are rich and they are the people who are corrupt. This is a country of ten millionaires and ten million poor people. We give people hope. We tell them that one day we shall form the government of this country. What we fight against is poverty, ignorance, diseases and bad governance.' Joe spoke with conviction. I found myself being swayed by his words.

When I had learned that I was to meet the Mungiki leadership, I didn't quite know what to expect. What I certainly *didn't* think would happen, though, was that I would come away feeling – at least partially – convinced by them. Of course, I didn't completely believe that the stories of Mungiki violence were nothing more than government propaganda. I knew that when they talked about giving the rude boys in the slums hope, chances were that the most those kids could hope for was that they didn't get their heads cut off. But they spoke eloquently and passionately about the poverty in which the people lived, about the corruption of the government, about the need for a welfare state and about their struggle against oppression. If these three were to be believed, the Mungiki's methods might be questionable, but their aims were admirable.

At the same time they were a scary trio. There was an intensity about them – Charles especially – that made me remain nervous about them despite the fact, or maybe because of it, that they said they would meet up with me again once I had done a bit more investigating.

I had heard about the Mungiki from both sides of the coin. What I wanted to do now was find somebody who could give me a balanced, objective view of them. That man was Maina Kiai, Chairman of the Kenyan National Commission on Human Rights. He had come under heavy criticism from the police and had also received death threats believed to be from the Mungiki. It sounded to me like he was in a pretty precarious position. It also sounded like he was happy to tell the truth about parties on both sides of the fence.

I was interested to know more about what the Mungiki had said about the government's neglect of the poor. Did anyone cater for them? Kiai was robust in his response. 'Nobody has. Governments and politicians talk the talk; they never walk it. They talk about it all the time, they talk about trying to bridge that gap, trying to care for the people. But we've had governments in this country where the leaders are much more preoccupied with themselves than with the people. Our MPs are some of the best paid in the world, despite the fact that we are in the bottom twenty-five countries in the UNDP Development Index. They give themselves a grant every five years to buy a vehicle for $50,000. They allocate themselves a gratuity of about $25,000 at the end of a five-year term. We have a group of greedy leaders, and that therefore means we find that security and everything else provided by the government stays with the rich and not with the poor. So the poor have been surviving by their wits.'

What Kiai was telling me didn't sound a million miles from what the Mungiki had to say. But what of the rumours which abounded about the Mungiki's methods? 'I don't know,' he said. 'There's no evidence to pinpoint the Mungiki to the beheadings, but that's the common assumption in this country. The other thing that's happened with Mungiki, as soon as they became a reviled group in this country, with almost every single major criminal activity the police would say it's Mungiki. So you find even non-Mungiki people extorting on the basis that they are Mungiki.'

Kiai spoke to me at length about the corruption of the government and the poverty of the people. He reiterated that the police in Kenya were little more than the government's bully boys, and that the main crisis in the country was one of security. From what he said, it was easy to see how vigilante groups might thrive. Kiai was articulate and passionate, and I left him thinking that Kenya would be a much happier place if he was in charge of it. He had also shed some light on why the Mungiki had such a fearsome reputation. Despite what he said, however, I still wasn't sure that they were entirely innocent of the accusations that were laid at their feet.

It was soon after my meeting with Maina Kiai that the Mungiki leadership got in touch again. They wanted to take me deeper into the slums of Nairobi, to show me the areas that they claim to have cleansed of crime and drugs. Dandora is an eastern suburb of Nairobi. It was built in 1977 with partial financing from the World Bank, but since then it has degenerated into a high-density slum. What distinguishes Dandora from other slums is the fact that it is also Nairobi's principal landfill site. It's a rubbish tip that stretches as far as the eye can see — it is fifteen square kilometres in size — and it has been named as one of the thirty most polluted sites in the world. That's a list that includes places such as Chernobyl. Nobody lives in Chernobyl any more, of course. They live in Dandora, though. They don't have much choice.

The rubbish tip swarms with people. There are even 'hotels' on the site, though these are little more than tents made out of sticks and rubbish bags where for a few shillings the impoverished can buy themselves a night's shelter and perhaps a bowl of decidedly unappetizing 'bone soup'. Many of the inhabitants of Dandora work the tips, sifting through the detritus in search of anything of value, or anything that can be recycled and sold on to the recycling plants. It's not much of a living, but it's something.

As soon as we arrived we had people coming up to us to tell us how much better this place was since the Mungiki took control. Before, it was rife with smaller gangs who would take money off the people working the tips; now those gangs have been moved off and everyone seems to be a lot happier. I guess these things are all a question of perspective — to me Dandora looked like hell on earth. Ragged people clamber over the piles of toxic rubbish. They have to fight for dominance with marabou storks, to my mind the ugliest birds in the world — balder than me and not much shorter. They can reach a metre and a half in height, and weigh up to nine kilos. They land on the tips and scavenge for food with their long beaks, seemingly oblivious to the humans there – or at least utterly unafraid of them. I had also been warned before we arrived that the tip was home to enormous toxic caterpillars that burn your skin if you touch them; plenty of people I saw had the marks to prove it. Dead rats litter the ground. At one stage I walked past a large stream of rainwater running off the rubbish tip. It was green with a grey scum. A truck drove past, and a small child fell off it and straight into the stream up to his waist. My every instinct was to wade in and help him, but I knew how toxic that water would be, and for a second I hesitated. Happily for him, the kid managed to scramble out. Happily for me, too.

I was shown around Dandora by Steven Njenga. I asked him how he had managed to take control of the area. 'Quite a lot of work has been done consistently for a long time,' he said as we wove our way through the piles of rubbish and the ragged people. 'You start with one person, you go and recruit another . . . you counsel them, you teach them to stop bad behaviour.'

He made it sound simple, but I wasn't so sure. I knew from past experience that if a gang owns a particular turf, taking that turf over is a hell of a sight more difficult than just bringing them round to your point of view.

Steven smiled at me. 'There is a divine call,' he said. 'Some things just happen miraculously. It's like a miracle.'

I told him I found that hard to believe, that I was a cynic.

'Then let's say there's a lot of work that is being done.'

As we headed deeper into Dandora, I couldn't deny that people certainly seemed hard at work. I wondered how it worked financially. Steven explained that a kilo of recyclable plastic was worth ten shillings. In the whole of Kenya 55,000 tons of plastic is discarded daily. Do the maths: there's a lot of shillings out there waiting to be collected. And this isn't the only way they make money. When Kenyan banknotes are printed, the offcuts of paper are dumped here. These are collected up, shredded, soaked and then spread out on mesh to make 'new' Manila paper, which is then sold on. Similarly, cigarette factories dump faulty cigarettes. The tobacco is taken, dried out if it needs to be, then rolled into new cigarettes for selling. It's amazing how many opportunities this landfill site presents to the desperate; and of course the Mungiki always take their cut. After all, they offer the 'protection'.

Steven arranged for me to meet a group of young men who worked in the dump site. There were perhaps twenty of them, all sitting calmly in a circle, and though their clothes were a good deal poorer than those of Steven and a couple of other Mungiki leaders who had joined us, they gave no sign of being dissatisfied with their lot. I asked the group how many of them used to be rude boys in Dandora. All of them, the answer came back. But now, as one of them – a lively-looking lad who I could well believe had been in his share of trouble – told me, they were converted. I don't know if the fact that they were surrounded by their Mungiki masters had anything to do with their unqualified praise of the organization, but they certainly seemed happy enough, more content with the Mungiki than with their previous masters – the government. They told me that not so long ago, in the period of a month, the Kenyan secret police, the Kwe Kwe, abducted twenty-five Mungiki members. Only two were recovered.

I left the dumping ground and walked into the actual town of Dandora. I wondered what the story would be if I spoke to people here when I didn't have the Mungiki leadership in tow. One man was willing to talk on camera. 'They're good people,' he said. 'They are very good people.' Off camera, though, it was a different story. Most of the inhabitants of this slum seemed too scared to talk to me about the Mungiki. I noticed a young woman selling fruit and veg on a street corner, and I could see that she was looking at me. I approached and asked her what she thought about the Mungiki.

'I can't talk to you about them,' she replied.

Why not?

'Because they will kill me.'

After a while you develop a kind of sixth sense that tells you if someone is being straight with you or not. That sense kicked in now: without doubt, this woman was scared for her life.

Dandora was a horrible place – though by all accounts it is a lot less horrible than it used to be. What I saw there, however, reinforced the opinion that was slowly forming in my mind. There was no way that the Mungiki had used gentle persuasion to cleanse this slum of the street gangs that had previously plagued it, and a significant proportion of the population was so scared of them that they refused even to talk to me. But there seemed to be a consensus, in certain parts of the community at least, that the arrival of the Mungiki had improved Dandora. And if the rude boys felt hard-done-by that their Mungiki masters wore better clothes and clearly had more money than them, they didn't show it. For myself, I was reminded of George Orwell's *Animal Farm*, and I started to wonder whether, in the eyes of the Mungiki, all Mungiki were equal, but some Mungiki were more equal than others.

I had witnessed the poverty that the Mungiki had vowed to fight, and I had to agree with them that it was a scourge that needed eradicating. Joe Waiganjo, however, had told me of another level to their activities: the political level. And we were in Kenya at a time of particular political unrest. Six months previously the general election had been held. After six years of unpopular government, the Kikuyu president, Kibaki, had been expected to lose power to his rival Raila Odinga. Widespread vote-rigging was reported. When Kibaki was declared the winner, the country erupted into violence. In protest against the rigged election, Kenya's other tribes – especially the Kalenjins, who had predominantly voted for Odinga – turned against the Kikuyus. In the violence that followed, 1,500 people died and 250,000 were driven from their homes.

It is too simplistic to say that the Mungiki are a Kikuyu gang, because although they are predominantly made up of lower-class Kikuyus, part of their struggle is against the Kikuyu elite that all but controls the government. Nevertheless, it was reported that the Mungiki were used as a militia to defend Kikuyus from the violence. The town of Eldoret, 300 kilometres north-west of Nairobi, saw some of the worst fighting. I went there to see if I could find out more about what had happened. I met up with a local journalist who explained to me what had been going on. 'Immediately after the election results were announced there was an abrupt eruption of violence. We saw people being beheaded by groups of youths from both sides. They were hacking each other – this happened even outside my own house.'

I had heard accusations that the Mungiki had told people in Kalenjin communities that if they didn't leave their houses in twenty-four hours they would kill the men and rape their wives.

'There were those complaints from the local community,'

my new journalist friend agreed. 'They had seen people being brought in from Nairobi direction and these people were heavily armed.'

Were they Mungiki or Kikuyu tribesmen?

'It is believed that some of them were Mungiki, considering the kinds of killings that were witnessed like the chopping off of heads, chopping off of private parts and displaying them publicly.'

Sounded familiar.

Kenya was coming to the brink of civil war: whole communities were ripped apart as people who had lived together for years suddenly became deadly enemies. The road to Eldoret bore shocking testament to what had happened. It was like teeth missing: rows of houses stopped abruptly, and there would be a gap where a Kikuyu house had formerly stood. These missing houses had not just been burned down, however; they had been removed stone by stone so that whoever lived in them could *never* return.

On New Year's Day the tribal violence reached a head at the Assemblies of God church just outside Eldoret when a group of Kikuyus was attacked by a Kalenjin mob. What happened that day shocked the world. We drove to the church, or what remained of it, to speak to the people involved. The site of the chapel was a wasteland. I was met there by Grace and Aroon, two survivors of the events of that day. The story they told me was absolutely horrific.

The Kikuyu community knew that an attack was coming, so they all decamped to the church for safety in numbers. They took their mattresses with them to sleep outside. The attack came at 11.00 a.m. The Kalenjin mob advanced, stopping now and then to sing a warlike song before advancing again. It was clear to the Kikuyus what the Kalenjin were doing: they were building up tension, instilling fear into their enemies and making it perfectly clear that they meant business.

When the Kalenjin finally fell upon them, the Kikuyu men tried to fight, but they were defeated. Six of them were hacked to death. The women and children – 350 of them – crammed into the tiny church. Thinking that they would be safe, that the mob wouldn't harm them, Aroon ran away and hid in an irrigation borehole. He was wrong about the Kalenjin mob's intentions, however. They piled the mattresses against the outside of the church, doused them in petrol, then set the church ablaze. Any Kikuyu trying to escape was hacked to death by the mob.

Grace tried to explain to me what the scene had been like inside the church. It's a description I'll never forget. 'We were like mad people,' she told me. 'I'm telling you, we were mad. I tried to throw a blanket against the fire. Me, I left here when the head of some kid had split. If you don't know, if a person burns the part which can split first is the head. I don't like to remember that kid, even today.' And at the very thought of it, Grace started to weep.

I could think of nothing to say to her.

Both Grace and Aroon lost children in the fire. It was impossible for me even to try and imagine what they had been through. As I wandered around the site of the atrocity, I saw that it was littered with the clothing of women and small children. With little shoes, burned and charred. Those few scraps of clothing were all that was left of innocent lives. Many people burned to death that day. They were put to the flame by people who were their friends and neighbours but who just happened to come from a different tribe. It beggared belief.

As a result of the post-election violence, whole communities had to flee their homes in fear of their lives. Consequently, NGOs from around the world have helped set up around 150 internally displaced persons camps, now home to approximately 300,000 people. One of these places was on the site of Eldoret Show Ground. It was a sea of white tents that just seemed to go on for ever. Most of the inhabitants of this sorry place were Kikuyus, unable to return home because their houses had been destroyed and because they knew that if they did, their lives were at risk. It was easy to understand, as I wandered around that temporary town of refugees, why organizations like the Mungiki thrived at times like this, and I was not surprised to learn that this was a prime recruiting ground for them.

My visit to Eldoret had been both shocking and eye-opening. But there was one more trip in store for me. I wanted to know more about what life was like on the streets in those parts of Kenya where the Mungiki did not have any influence. The slums of Mathari and Dandora had been bad, but I had been told of a place that was a grade lower than that, a place where people on the very bottom rung of society lived. The Mungiki had told me that it was their mission to bring hope to people who had none; what I was about to see embodied hopelessness like I had never witnessed, and the like of which I hope never to see again.

On the outskirts of Eldoret there is a rubbish tip. This is where the glue kids live. There are 350,000 homeless children in Kenya. In the West well-meaning people donate money to sponsor children in deprived areas such as this. The reality, as one charity worker in Kenya told me, is that very little of the money gets through to the children who need it so badly. Often the letters that the sponsors receive in return for their cash are written in batches, all of them the same. They make the sponsors feel better, but they're not from the kids they are supposed to be helping, and their money is being stolen. So despite these people's best efforts, it's still tough being a street kid in Kenya, and the really unlucky ones end up here.

The glue kids are addicted to solvents, to the glue that is used all over the world. Children barely old enough to walk have the little plastic bottles clamped to their lips, breathing in the fumes from the solvents to give them the hit to which they are chemically addicted. Walking among them was like walking into Dante's inferno. I saw mothers giving glue bottles to their toddlers; I saw tiny children adept at placing a stick into their bottle to release some more fumes from the glue; I saw one woman so high on solvents that she bent over and dropped the baby she was carrying on its head. The woman just smiled dreamily and then performed a little dance – I don't know if she even realized what had happened. She then picked the toddler up and put the glue fumes to its mouth to stop it crying.

It was a genuinely heartbreaking scene. I wanted to talk to one of these children, and a particular kid caught my eye. His name was Alex, and like all the others he was inhaling deeply from a bottle of glue. He said he was eleven years old, but he looked a good deal younger. I asked him how long he had been on the streets. 'Two years,' he told me. He had ended up here because his mother was addicted to alcohol, and he had started sniffing glue one year ago.

I asked him if he wanted to keep doing it. 'No,' he told me, his eyes wide and his voice gentle and faltering. 'It hurts my chest.'

If he had the opportunity of leaving the streets, what would he like to do? 'To go to school,' he said plaintively.

I wanted to take little Alex home with me. At the very least I wanted to do something to help him. But in a place like that you can't just give a young kid money because it will be stolen from him within seconds. In any case, it's unfair to help one child and not all the others. We couldn't stand by and do nothing, however, so I arranged for him to be taken off and given a decent meal. It wasn't much, and afterwards we had to return him to the glue community, but at least we had made his life a little bit easier, if only for a couple of hours. Nevertheless, I knew the future was grim for Alex. Whether he is still alive now, I simply don't know.

I've seen some shocking things on my travels. I've seen some hopeless, desperate places. But nowhere has moved me more than that helpless, forgotten community. It was perfectly obvious to any right-minded observer that something had to be done about it; it was equally obvious from what I had learned that these children were low on the government's agenda. I was beginning to understand just how the Mungiki might be able to garner support in such places.

What I saw during my time in Eldoret helped me understand why the Mungiki might feel compelled to help their fellow Kikuyus, even if it didn't justify the brutal means by which they were rumoured to do so. It was becoming clear to me, however, that the layers of politics, enmity and inter-tribe rivalry that existed in Kenyan society were extremely complicated. Too complicated for an outsider like me to understand? Quite possibly.

One thing was sure, though: the more I learned about the Mungiki and the morally uncertain world in which they lived, the less I felt qualified to judge them.

By this time the Mungiki leadership seemed to trust me. We had been allowed unprecedented access to them and to their projects in the slums – albeit always under their watchful eye. Now they were going to allow us to take one step further into their midst. I was invited to join them – and sixty new recruits – for a secret ritual up in the central highlands of Kenya, their spiritual homeland. What we were about to witness was an initiation ceremony, and it was the first time they had ever allowed anyone to film it. The highlands of Kenya are beautiful – a far cry from the urban slums of Nairobi. They are also bloody cold, at least they are at dawn, which was when the ceremony was to take place. Very little was known about this ritual, and as I arrived I had no idea what to expect.

It was a quiet, serious affair. If you didn't know what was going on, you would have thought it was a traditional religious service. Allegiances were intoned by a 'minister' and repeated by the recruits, who all had their arms raised in the air, palms outwards, as they prayed towards Mount Kenya. A lamb was brought in and slaughtered by Charles Ndungu, the acting leader of the Mungiki, its throat cut with a sharp knife and its body surrounded by eucalyptus leaves; the blood was drained into a bowl and salt added to stop it coagulating. The lamb itself was skinned, butchered and taken off to be boiled – all the new recruits had been given the promise of a little meat if they joined up. I was given a taste – a great honour, no doubt, but not a great culinary revelation. I think I'll be sticking to the rosemary and garlic treatment in the future.

As the sun rose, the young men filed calmly and serenely down the hill towards a freezing-cold river pool, where they were to be baptized. There was a genuine sense of peace about the place, and it was clear that the recruits were taking their initiation very seriously indeed. The quasi-biblical ceremony itself was all part of Maina Njenga's vision for the Mungiki. The young men were completely immersed in the icy water, and as they emerged from the pool they were rubbed with special oils and creams. These substances were displayed to me with a sense of hushed reverence. 'Clove oil! Coconut oil!' To hear them speak, you would think I was being shown the rarest treasures on earth; in fact, they were little more than moisturizing creams you could find in any supermarket.

It would be easy to deride the ceremony, but the truth is that for the young men being initiated into the Mungiki this was obviously a very emotional occasion. It meant a hell of a lot to them. As they wandered off into the early-morning mist, I was left to reflect that like all new initiates into gangs of every kind, these people had just been given something: a sense of community, of strength in numbers. And in a country where the poor are as oppressed as they are in Kenya, that's a very powerful thing indeed.

All in all the Mungiki ceremony was a peaceful – if intense – experience. The authorities, however, clearly didn't see it in the same light. A little more than an hour after we left the site, thirty-eight armed police turned up. I don't suppose they'd arrived to congratulate the new recruits on the occasion of their baptism, but happily, by that time, we were well away.

Not long afterwards a piece of information reached us. It was bad news for the Mungiki, and even as we heard, it was clear to us that, if true, it could be the catalyst for something big. Maina Njenga's wife – the woman who had been at his house when I first met the Mungiki leadership – had been abducted along with her driver. The driver had managed to get a call out to his cousin, and the last thing that was heard was the sound of him pleading for his life. Back in Nairobi I had the sense of a city holding its breath. Everyone knew that if these rumours were true, there would be repercussions. And if Maina Njenga's wife had been killed, so much the worse . . .

In the meantime, we were granted access by the Mungiki to a remarkable – and rather spooky – woman. Her name was Florence, and before she was 'saved' by Maina Njenga's cause and the Mungiki, she had been by her own admission a bad girl. 'A *very* bad girl.' Florence had been a prostitute for fifteen years and admitted to being involved in all sorts of crime. Now, however, she claimed to have seen the light and was one of the Mungiki's best recruiters – and had consequently been labelled the most wanted woman in Kenya. Florence lived in a top-secret safe house deep in the Nairobi slums – so secret that we were not allowed to interview her there. Instead, we had to bring Florence to us. She had with her a Mungiki guard. He was meant to be keeping an eye on her and, we assumed, ensuring that she didn't say anything she wasn't supposed to. We got lucky, however. When the guard was offered a cup of tea and a piece of cake, the temptation was too much and he went off to claim his free snack. It gave me the opportunity to ask Florence anything I wanted. The interview ended up being deeply revealing.

Florence was a striking-looking woman. She had high cheekbones and attractive brown hair that fell down in ringlets. But there was an intensity to her eyes. A kind of fire that spoke of the passion she felt for the Mungiki cause. A look like that unnerves you the moment you see it, and you instantly know you're in the company of a deeply unpredictable person. I knew that I, for one, wouldn't want to meet her in a dark alley.

I asked Florence what exactly she did for the Mungiki cause. 'I'm a coordinator,' she said, speaking English in her African accent with a clear, fervent precision, 'of women. I change their life within thirty minutes.' She smiled and stared at me.

How did she do that, I asked.

'I read them Bible and tell them, "I was like you one day. One day I was a bad girl."'

Did she specifically target prostitutes?

'Yes. And even thieves. I talk to them and I love them. So I can change about thirty per day. Maina Njenga changed my life. I was a bad girl. I was smoking very much *bang* [marijuana]. I've been jailed because of robbery. I was even slaughtering girls.'

She laughed slightly as she told me that. I wanted to make sure I had fully understood her. 'You killed people?' I asked.

'Yeah. I was brewing *changaa*. I was selling to people, and if you don't pay me I was taking a glass and slaughter you. I could do everything to you. So everyone was fearing me.'

I had heard rumours that some of the girls who join the Mungiki underwent female circumcision. Was that true?

'Yes,' she sighed almost rapturously. 'Of course. And it's not bad. It's Kikuyus' culture.'

But was it true, as I had heard, that some women were locked up and *forced* to undergo circumcision?

'Not forced,' Florence told me emphatically. 'No. That's lies. It is your wish. Now, in April, there are twenty girls. They come to my house.'

I wasn't sure how much detail I wanted to know about the procedure, but I had to ask the question: how was it done?

'There is an old woman,' Florence told me. 'She will come with a knife and I just take a paper bag. I'll take the legs of the girl, and then I'll cover the neck like this.' She made an X shape with her arms across her chest. 'I say

199

please, please, please hold on. And then the mama, she just cuts. It's just a small thing. Just a very small thing.'

I pointed out that some people might disagree with her about that.

She smiled broadly. 'Just a very small thing,' she reiterated.

But doesn't it mean that the woman won't be able to enjoy sex in the future?

'That's lies,' Florence retorted. 'To be circumcized is a good thing. That is what I do believe, because I can stay about three years without a man, and I can survive. But uncircumcized girls can't stay, because when that thing stand like this, you feel it and you want a man. You can be fucked by everybody, even dogs!' Florence started to cackle at the thought. Something she had just said really amused her. I didn't know what it was.

I felt I wanted to change the subject. 'We hear that the Mungiki go into the slums and remove the pickpockets and clear up the streets. How do they do that?'

'It's just to tell you,' Florence replied, 'if I see you one day pickpocketing here, I take off your head.' She laughed again.

And if she saw them again, *would* she cut their heads off?

'I'd have to take you,' she replied. 'If I saw you pick-pocketing, I wouldn't allow you. I'd take you to my place.'

Then what?

'I'll beat you. Or I'll tell you, just put your hands up. I'll leave you free.'

There was something rather terrifying about Florence's words and her demeanour. She was trying to make herself sound firm but kind, I think; I had no doubt, however, that she'd strike the fear of God into anyone she dealt with.

I asked her if the Mungiki had been involved in any of the post-election violence. In an instant she looked away in disgust, as though she were offended by the very question. 'No,' she spat. 'I was sleeping. Sleeping and laughing. Enjoying.'

Why was she laughing while people were being killed?

'Because he had told them about this. These people deny it. They were told by Maina: one day you will be killed here. Come and wash your body, be baptized – you won't be killed. They refused. They say Maina is a crazy boy, what is he telling us? Now, they were asking, where is Maina? The boy told us the truth now – see, we are living in the camps! So I was laughing!'

I wondered what Florence thought of the abduction of Maina Njenga's wife. She became grave and screwed up her eyes. 'My blood is telling me they are dead,' she pronounced.

Who did she think was responsible?

'These were not thieves,' she said. There was no doubt in her voice. 'Just policemen.'

Kwe Kwe – the secret police?

'Yes. Yes. They want us to feel pain so that we can leave Mungiki. So Maina can stay alone, get stranded. But even if they take my baby, and kill my baby, I'll never go back.' Florence shook her head emphatically, and I believed what she was saying. '*Never.* Mungiki are everywhere in Kenya. Everywhere.' She started reeling off a list of cities, her voice getting more and more excited as she did so. 'Even in the office of the vice president, there are Mungiki there. He doesn't know. In universities, primary schools, secondary schools – *full* of Mungiki!' Florence's eyes shone at the thought. 'Street boys, all for Maina!'

And what would happen, I asked, if someone killed Maina Njenga?

Florence fixed me with a piercing stare. 'It would be blood-shed,' she said, her voice quiet now, but more menacing for it. 'We will revenge the whole world. Mombasa, Eldoret, everywhere – we'll burn the houses to hell. And I'll be in front.'

She continued to stare at me, calmly, but with a fervour in her eyes bordering on madness. It was the stare of a true zealot, and I did not doubt a single word of what she had said.

It was shortly after I met Florence that the car in which Maina Njenga's wife had been travelling was found by the Tanzanian border – a very long way from Nairobi. In the woods just outside the capital four bodies were uncovered. Two of them had been there for a long time and were unrecognizable – in Africa bodies left out in the open soon get eaten by wild animals. The other two had been attacked, and it could still be discerned what had happened to them. They were a man and woman. The male had been smashed in the head with a blunt instrument that had crushed the back of his skull. The woman had been tied up with wire – she had wire cuts around her ankles and wrists. She had been raped several times. She had knife cuts all over her body that suggested she had been tortured. And her throat had been cut so severely that she was almost decapitated. Despite the fact that her body had been so brutalized, it was still possible to identify her as Virginia Njenga.

It seemed Florence's instincts had been right.

In the aftermath of the killing, the police claimed that it was down to infighting among the Mungiki. The Mungiki claimed that it was the Kwe Kwe who had carried out the assassination. I can't say for sure which of them was telling the truth, but I'm more inclined to believe one side than the other.

Two days later Kenya awoke to the backlash.

It started before sunrise. All over Kenya Mungiki took to the streets, setting fire to vehicles and blocking roads. It quickly brought the country to a standstill, leaving nobody in any doubt about how angry the Mungiki were. And we were caught right in the middle of it. We had made it our business to find out what was happening. The Mungiki, it transpired, had hijacked lorries and buses. Some of them they set fire to; others they parked across the main roads and then let the air out of the tyres. As a result, the roads into Nairobi were crammed with vehicles, abandoned because it was clear that nobody was going anywhere; the roads out were deserted. On the outskirts of the city, in our attempts to negotiate the unnavigable streets, we turned down a side road – and straight into the path of an angry mob.

They were about a hundred metres away and closing in on us fast. From the noise they were making, they didn't sound at all friendly. I could sense the whole camera team was nervous; I was nervous too, and I shouted at everyone to get back in the cars. There was a scramble as we tried to hide ourselves from the mob. Our African drivers seemed even more scared than us – I guess they had a better sense of what could happen – and they turned the cars round quickly, ready for us to make our escape. 'Faster!' they urged as we clambered into the cars. 'Faster! Faster!'

Opening the front passenger window, I could see them approaching even closer. They were holding pickaxe handles and small axes and a few had machetes or *pangas*. One thing was clear, though: these guys weren't messing around.

Then, from nowhere, I felt a sense of defiance. Some people might call it stupidity. 'Fuck it,' I murmured to myself, and I opened the door.

From inside the car I heard the voice of reason. 'Just stay here, okay, Ross?' someone said. But I didn't. I climbed out of the car, put my hands in the air and walked towards the mob. I don't really know what I thought would happen – it's not like I have much experience handling situations like this, and I couldn't even tell if it was a Mungiki mob or Kalenjins out looking for Kikuyus. Furthermore, because most film crews in Kenya are in the employ of the government, they often get attacked. All in all, this wasn't the best moment for a show of misplaced bravery, especially as once I'd decided to take the plunge, the camera crew felt they had to follow. And so I led them into what could have been a very ugly situation. Incidentally Will, the cameraman, and Kiff, the sound technician, still laugh about it to this day.

As I approached, the crowd unfurled a banner. 'Government,' it read, 'stop these extra-judicial killings.'

I stopped a few metres away from the mob and made a placating gesture to them. To my relief, they fell silent. I asked them if they were complaining because Njenga's wife had been killed. 'Yes!' they shouted together. They wanted Njenga free. They wanted the government to stop killing innocent citizens. I asked if they admitted to being Mungiki. 'Yes!' they shouted again.

'No more killing!' someone called from the crowd, and a few others took up the mantra. 'No more killing! No more killing!' The mob started getting excited again. They moved on. 'Without Njenga there is no peace in Kenya!' they shouted, and as they carried on down the road I saw nothing to suggest they were going to calm down any time soon.

We followed the mob, knowing that sooner or later they would meet the police. I had already seen what could happen in such situations, and talking to one of the crowd made it clear to me that they were under no illusions about the risk they were taking. 'When they arrest us, when they take you to the police station, they kill you. Hanging.' He made a throat-cutting gesture to illustrate his point. Despite the dangers, though, this mob was on the rampage. The Mungiki had closed down Nairobi, they were angry and they were going to make their voices heard.

The air was filled with angry shouts and with thick black smoke from burning tyres. And then there was the unmistakable sound of a gunshot from a GSU truck coming up the road. We now followed the police towards a small group of dwelling places where crowds were congregating. The police continued to fire rounds and threw tear-gas grenades towards the people, who scurried away like ants from the billowing clouds of chemicals. The GSU alighted from their vehicles and started taking charge of the area, locking and loading their guns and barking instructions through a loud-speaker. 'Go home! Go to your houses!' More truckloads of police arrived: they had the area cleared soon enough.

Twenty members of the Mungiki were shot by police as a result of the riots. The Kenyan police had been after their blood, and they'd got it. As a result, the Mungiki leaders had to go into hiding. That night I went to see them at another safe house for a final meeting, where I didn't get the impression that they felt very safe at all.

The place where we met was little more than a shack. I was scared as I sat at a small table with Steven Njenga and Joe Waiganjo. These were wanted men, and if the police caught up with them, they'd be killed – and it wouldn't matter who got caught in the crossfire. As before it was Joe who did most of the talking. I wanted to know how Maina Njenga had reacted to the death of his wife. 'He is very, very bitter,' Joe told me, his voice grave. 'He has decided to go on a hunger strike, of which we are highly supportive. He is using Mahatma Gandhi-style peaceful resistance. What they are trying to do is eliminate the leadership of our party.

Let's hope to God that they don't do so, because if they *do* do so, what will be experienced in Kenya I'm sure they will not be able to handle.'

This meeting was my last chance to make some sense of the different opinions I had heard about the Mungiki during my stay here. I expressed my belief that there were many decent people in the organization, but that there were also criminals. For one final time, I asked them: do they use violence to achieve their ultimate goal?

'No,' Joe told me emphatically, and he had nothing else to say on the subject. 'The government will not be able to crush us,' he said. 'Whether we die or not, the movement will still live on and the party will still see its light of day. And one day, Ross Kemp, we will welcome you when we are in the government.'

Joe spoke calmly. It was a calmness that belied the Mungiki leadership's situation, and I wanted to know how much danger he was really in.

'Personally,' he told me, his voice perfectly level, 'I am at the fear of being killed any moment. I may die even twenty minutes from now.' And as the meeting came to an end, he delivered a stark warning: 'If we were to disappear, do not look for us. Just know we are dead.'

Joe Waiganjo's haunting parting words were truer than I realized at the time. In the light of the riots and the civil disorder that we had just witnessed, the Kenyan authorities asked for a meeting with the Mungiki leadership. Charles Ndungu, whom I had come to know during my stay in Kenya, was due to attend. Before meeting the government, he set off for the prison where Maina Njenga was being held to seek his leader's advice and make sure he was singing from the same hymn sheet. On the way, his car was ambushed.

Nineteen bullets flew into his vehicle and a number of them struck his body. Charles died instantly.

The government's official line was that Charles had been killed as a result of infighting in the Mungiki leadership. But in all the time I had been with them I had seen no sign of tension or disagreement. On the contrary, they seemed of one mind. Maybe I had got the wrong end of the stick; maybe they had pulled the wool over my eyes. Or maybe not. It isn't up to me to say who killed Charles Ndungu. All I can do is observe the facts. There seems little doubt that the government knew Charles was going to meet Njenga. He was ambushed by people with machine guns on the way to that meeting. He knew the government had no love for his organization. And, like the other members of the Mungiki leadership, he always knew that death could be just around the corner. You can draw your own conclusions from that.

I could never have guessed when I first arrived in Kenya that I would be allowed such unprecedented access to the Mungiki, or that I would have arrived at such a pivotal and turbulent time for them. I could certainly never have guessed that by the time I left two of the people I would meet would have been brutally murdered. But murder is commonplace in Kenya. Maybe I shouldn't have been surprised.

If I learned nothing else in Kenya, I learned this: nothing is straightforward. In a country with mass poverty and endemic corruption, the Mungiki appear to offer something where there is nothing. I had heard good things about them, and very bad things. I had no way of proving or disproving any of them. What was clear, however, was that despite countless efforts by self-serving governments to wipe them out, they appear to be thriving. Whether the Mungiki truly use the power they have for the good of the people or for their own gain, I have no idea. Nevertheless, it was certainly true that many of them were prepared to sacrifice their own lives for the chance of something better.

If forced to an opinion, I would have to say that my impression was that the Mungiki had the best intentions, but that these intentions were sometimes perverted by people inside their structure. I think that despite their denials they sometimes use violence to achieve their ends, and while I would never condone that, I stop short of judging them for it. Africa is a violent place, and the poor of Kenya have a profoundly difficult life; to judge them by our Western standards is impossible.

Perhaps the last word should be given to Maina Kiai, the Chairman of the Kenyan National Commission on Human Rights, whom I had met earlier in my stay. 'There are two tribes in Kenya and in Africa,' he told me. 'The rich and the poor. One's a very small tribe, the other's a very big one.'

He's right. And while that remains the case, there will always be a place for organizations like the Mungiki.

6. Liverpool

Over the past few years my search for the world's toughest gangs has taken me all around the world. I've travelled to six different continents, ending up in places I barely knew existed, meeting people I never thought I'd meet and seeing sights, frankly, that I hope never to see again. Gangsterism is a worldwide phenomenon. But the truth is that you don't have to take a plane halfway round the world to witness it. A quick trip up the M6 is all you need.

I love Liverpool. Its people are great, its architecture is fantastic and everyone has a brilliant sense of humour. After London, it's my favourite city in the UK. Aside from their warmth and wit, Liverpudlians have a deep sense of pride in their city. It's okay if you're a Scouser to take the piss out of Liverpool, but woe betide anyone else who does. It's an attitude I can understand – I'm from Essex, after all! – but Liverpudlians have good reason for this sense of pride in their city. It's not just that it's a world heritage site; it's not just that they gave us the Beatles. Liverpool has always been, and to this day remains, one of the most important cities in Britain.

Historically speaking, there's a very good reason for this: water. Liverpool is a busy port, and in an island nation that gives it a certain standing. The Port of Liverpool has always been an important gateway, and not only to those importing legitimate goods. Britain's ports have been a hotbed of contraband for hundreds of years, making them magnets for criminality. Liverpool is no exception to this. It's a well-connected place with a long history of crime and a long history of gangs.

As far back as 1886 the Liverpool *Daily Post* wrote about the matter. 'The highest type of civilization and the lowest type of savagery are to be found in Liverpool, existing side by side; and in no city in the world can a more startling contrast of the two races of mankind – the civilized and the uncivilized – be found.' The event that gave rise to this outburst was a gang killing. On 3 August 1874 a law-abiding worker by the name of Richard Morgan, along with his brother Samuel and wife Alice, was stopped by four or five members of the notorious High Rip gang, who demanded 'six pence for a quart of ale'. History does not record exactly what Richard Morgan's response was, though it's not hard to imagine what it *might* have been. The gang immediately attacked him. He fell to the floor, where his wife tried to help him, but one of the gangsters started choking Morgan. Alice herself was punched in the ear, rendering her deaf. As she screamed for help, a mob gathered round and encouraged the gang. Richard Morgan's body was kicked all the way down the street. When a policeman finally arrived, the gang dispersed, but it was too late. Richard Morgan was dead.

The event, which became known as the Tithebarn Street Outrage, made national news and brought to public attention the gang problem that existed in Liverpool at the time. The High Rip was the most feared and notorious of the Liverpool gangs, but it was not the only one. They were bitter enemies with an outfit which called itself the Logwood gang, and there were lesser groups such as the Lemon Street gang and the Housebreakers, all of them terrorizing the streets of the city centre. And while they may not have been packing Glocks, the murder of Richard Morgan shows how violent they were.

In his book *The Gangs of Liverpool* Michael Macilwee points out that even in those days opinion was divided as to the best way to deal with the gang problem. Some members of the public urged the building of new housing for this violent minority, and suggested the best way to deal with the gangsters was to buy them some food and reason with them – a kind of precursor to 'hug-a-hoodie'. Others thought harsher deterrents and tougher sentences were the only solution. It's sad how little things change.

Or maybe they do. Because when I visited Liverpool to investigate the modern gang culture that most assuredly exists there I saw some new approaches to the gang problem – some good, some questionable. But I also saw plenty to be worried about. And in the year when Liverpool is the European Capital of Culture, I saw a culture of a very different kind. A gun culture. A culture of disrespect for authority. A culture of violence that has culminated in crimes that have shocked the nation and aren't a million miles away from the murder of Richard Morgan more than a century ago.

Croxteth, L11. To look at it, you would never think that this northern suburb of Liverpool is a hotbed of gang violence. It's hardly a well-to-do part of town – certainly it's not the jewel in Liverpool's crown – but it's pleasant enough. There are flowers in the front gardens and cars parked outside houses. You can tell just by looking at it that the inhabitants of Croxteth take pride in where they live, and the overwhelming majority of them are decent, respectable folk. But there's no getting away from the fact that Croxteth has a reputation, and it was here, in August 2007, that an event happened which horrified everyone who heard about it. Rhys Jones, a happy, football-crazy, eleven-year-old boy, was on his way home from soccer training, still wearing his kit, when he was shot dead outside the Fir Tree pub. Rhys Jones's murder was a terrible moment in Liverpool's history, an incident that shattered the community where it happened. It was not, however, the only episode of gun violence this part of the city had seen in recent years. Far from it.

Norris Green is Croxteth's neighbouring suburb. They are divided by a single main road and to look at the two areas you'd be hard pushed to find much in the way of difference between them – or, indeed, between them and many other parts of the country. In Norris Green, about a mile or so away from where Rhys Jones was killed, there's a pub that used to be called the Royal Oak. When I walked in there I didn't sense that it was a particularly rough place – it's the sort of joint where you'd be perfectly happy to sit and have a quiet pint – but in the early hours of 1 January 2004, just as a New Year's Eve party started winding down, it became part of Liverpool's gang folklore.

On the night in question a masked man entered the function room, where nineteen-year-old Danny McDonald was sitting, pulled out a gun and shot him. Everyone in the pub ducked for cover. Danny, amazingly, managed to stagger as far as the door before collapsing dead. No one was ever charged with his murder. This was no random killing. The police could tell immediately from the nature of the crime that Danny McDonald most likely knew his murderer, and it was not lost on anyone that he had a reputation as one of the leaders of the Croxteth – or 'Croccy' – crew.

Fast-forward two years. At the nearby Altcourse Prison a young man called Liam 'Smigger' Smith is visiting a friend who's doing time. He gets into an argument with another man. As Smigger leaves, the man is overheard saying to an inmate, 'Quick, quick, give us the phone; I'll get the lads to pop them.' A convoy leaves Croxteth and, as Smigger exits the prison's visiting centre, a gunman jumps out of the bushes and shoots him in the face with a sawn-off shotgun. It is thought that these tit-for-tat gang killings ultimately led to the death of Rhys Jones, and the streets of Liverpool resound with rumours. Any more than that I cannot say for legal reasons.

The funeral of Liam Smith was one of the largest Norris Green had ever winessed. He was seen by many as a soldier, a casualty of the bitter war between the Norris Green Strand gang and the Croxteth Crew. Four people were eventually sentenced to a total of eighty-six years for his murder. One of them, a sixteen-year-old with an IQ of 71, was jailed for life.

It was not the first time I had been struck by the young age of the people involved in gang violence, but things are always a bit more shocking the closer they are to your front door. We hear a lot these days about the antisocial behaviour of our young people, but I don't think it's a new phenomenon and I'm not alone in having had my moments of waywardness as a kid. There is something eye-opening, however, about a life sentence for a sixteen-year-old, and I can't help wondering if the prospect of such a punishment is a meaningful deterrent for someone who, at such a young age, is yet to have a life and so has no way of knowing what it means to take one or have their own taken away.

One thing was sure, though. If I wanted to find out more about the gangs of Liverpool, it seemed that Croxteth and Norris Green would be the places to start my investigation.

There was no doubt that the inhabitants of these two suburbs didn't want me or the film crew on their turf. Why would they? They were clearly worried that the whole community was going to be tarred with the same brush as the criminal minority. One guy went so far as to accuse me of having gone round the streets of Croxteth offering £100 to anybody who said they were a gang member. These are accusations that we have to take very seriously and we dealt with it legally, but to some extent I can understand why people would want to do this: to protect their neighbourhood, to stop it being stereotyped. In this part of Liverpool, however, the stereotype already exists. When I arrived in L11 I hooked up with Chris Neil, a photo-journalist and gang expert who knows the area well. I asked him just how bad the problem was.

'I've been seeing gun crime all over the UK for twenty years, and Liverpool 11 – I've not seen anything like it. It's got its two factions, Noggses [Norris Green] and Croccy Crew [Croxteth]. Jointly, the two gangs have got about fifty members, twenty-five in each, or somewhere thereabouts.'

These weren't big numbers, but that didn't mean it wasn't a big problem. I wondered what was the origin of the two gangs' enmity. Why were they at each other's throats?

'It's a very good question,' Chris replied. 'I just don't see what the reason is here. I don't see what the end is. There's no major drugs battle – it's not as if you can say there's these pubs and there's those pubs where there are protection rackets.' None of the usual reasons, then, for violence between communities.

Together we drove through Croxteth, and Chris pointed out the school where all the gang members went. 'It's amazing,' he said. 'You've got forty or fifty kids all bordering on gang warfare that grew up as children together.' It was certainly a strange scenario. There seemed to be no reason for this divisive hatred. I wondered if I might be able to find out more. Chris didn't sound very hopeful. 'One thing that they have in common, other than the fact that they're extremely violent and they wear the same clothes, is they have a strict code of silence. Both factions. They will not grass on each other.'

A code of silence. I was worried that this might be an obstacle in my quest to get close to some of the youth gangs of the city. Just a couple of days in, however, we got a lucky break. A group of gang members from Norris Green agreed to meet me at a secret location; what was more, they agreed to bring with them some of the weapons they used in their ongoing war with the Croccy Crew.

I never got to see the faces of the Norris Green gang members. They all wore what appeared to be almost a regulation uniform: black trousers, black hoods and their faces covered by the high collars of their black anoraks. Consequently I couldn't tell by looking at them how old they were. Their voices, though, did not sound exactly elderly. As I interviewed them they sat in a line. Two of them carried samurai swords; a third was wielding an evil-looking weapon consisting of two curved blades shaped like horns around a central handle. It was the sort of thing you might expect to see in a medieval armoury, not in the fist of a young man from Liverpool in the twenty-first century.

I asked them what would happen if one of the Croxteth Crew walked in at that moment. They answered almost in unison. 'We'd chop his head off. Stick this through his neck. And then I'd still carry on stabbing him even though his head weren't still on his neck.' Without seeing their faces, it was difficult to judge how much of this was bravado, but their voices were dripping with contempt and aggression. You certainly wouldn't want to be a Croxteth lad alone in the presence of these guys.

I wanted to understand where this hatred came from. I put it to them that there wasn't much in the way of a drugs trade in the area, and they agreed with me. 'There was at one time,' I was told, 'but it's dying down now.'

Did they know *why* it was dying down? 'Because the people involved,' they told me, 'have all been nicked. Or shot.'

And had any of them ever been shot at?

'Yes,' they all replied immediately and at the same time. One of them had actually been hit in the top of his leg. It went through the bone and broke his leg. He didn't know exactly what weapon had been used to shoot him, but he thought it was a nine-millimetre pistol.

So if they weren't fighting over drugs, what *were* they fighting over? What was at the root of it all?

'It's just gangs. Two fucking different gangs, both arguing. It's like that everywhere in the world. Two gangs always fighting.'

And do they see any end to it?

'No. There won't be an end unless everyone fucking dies.'

They sounded pretty sure about that. With that thought in mind, I wanted to know how easy it was for a young gang member in Britain today to get their hands on a gun. How would they go about doing it?

'Phone someone,' they answered evasively. 'Get it dropped off or go and pick it up.'

And how long would that take?

'About five minutes, if that.' They seemed confident that they could put their hands on any firearm they wanted from a nine-millimetre pistol to a shotgun to assault weapons. The idea of street gangsters in Liverpool packing AK-47s was a sobering one.

I wondered if they used drugs. 'Only on the weekend,' they told me. And only marijuana. What about the harder stuff? Is there any crack out there, any smack? 'We don't touch that,' they told me forcefully. But people take it in the area. 'There's smackheads everywhere.' The gang members' opinions of such people, like most of their opinions, were robust. 'Horrible scumbags. Kill them too. We always give them loads when we see them.'

I wanted to know what the lads thought of the police. How did they behave in the area? What did the gangs think of them? The answer, I suppose, was predictable enough. 'Scumbags. Bastards. They just can't stand us. They really hate us.'

And what about the future? Did they see the gang situation in Croxteth and Norris Green improving or getting worse. 'Worse. There's going to be more and more kids growing up who want to fight. The kids are getting worse.'

They didn't say this with any sense of glee; there was a resigned tone to their voices, as if they had just accepted that this was the situation. A couple of them suggested that things might be improved if there were more football pitches and green spaces for kids to go to, but I knew this was a bit disingenuous. There *were* such places in the area, but in order to get to them, the Noggses would have to cross through certain areas where they knew they would come under attack.

But what if they had the chance to make their voices heard? What if the Home Secretary was sitting in front of them? What would they like to say to her?

There was an awkward pause. 'Who?'

'The Home Secretary. The woman in charge of the police force.'

'Fucking spit at her. Call her a scumbag. They wouldn't listen to a word we have to say. Tell her to stop picking on the kids and make the streets better. It just sends them mad, all the bizzies [police] jumping out on them constantly.'

My chat with the Noggsy crew had been a frustrating one

in some ways. They weren't unintelligent, but they couldn't explain at all convincingly why they had such a hatred for their Croxteth counterparts. Perhaps unwittingly, however, they had revealed more than they intended. They were very much a product of their environment. Their vicious hatred of crackheads and smackheads was telling. During the 1980s drug addiction in Britain tripled. In Liverpool there was so much heroin on the streets that it became known as Smack City. Areas like Croxteth and Norris Green were devastated by the problem; families were torn apart by addiction. I have no way of knowing how many of the young men I interviewed that day had been personally affected by the 80s heroin explosion, but you don't have to be a social historian to work out why they might have such a violent hatred of hard drugs.

I thought it was also significant that they had no idea who the Home Secretary was. They hated authority, loathed the police and knew nothing about politics: these gang members were disenfranchisement personified.

But what was most alarming was the casual way they spoke about firearms. Guns were no big deal to them – just an ordinary part of their everyday lives. They could get hold of them easily, and they were obviously fully prepared to use them. As I returned to the centre of Liverpool and saw the waterfront, I was reminded of Liverpool's port status. The swords and blades that the Noggses were brandishing hadn't entered this country by plane; nor had the assault weapons they claimed to be able to put their hands on so easily. They had surely come in by boat, and as one of the busiest ports in the country, Liverpool was ideally placed to take delivery.

The police, of course, are fully aware of this problem. The day after I met the Norris Green gang, I went to visit a specialist police unit that has been set up with tackling gangs and gun crime in particular. It's called the Matrix and it's run by Inspector Steve Morris. Steve prepared for me a little display of the kind of weapons that they had confiscated from the streets of Liverpool. Fourteen different firearms were laid out on a table before me. It was quite an arsenal, from pistols to assault weapons. The idea of any of these guns in the young hands of the gangsters of L11 was a frightening one.

Steve Morris highlighted for me one of the major problems the Matrix unit faces. Half the weapons laid out in front of me, he explained, were the real deal. The other half were toys or replicas. 'I would challenge anybody,' he said, 'in a split second to decide which is real and which is an imitation – which is intended as a child's toy and which is intended to take a life. And sometimes police officers have to make that decision within literally a split second.'

The point was well made. I picked up what looked like a Heckler and Koch assault rifle. It weighed about the same as the real thing; at a glance, to all intents and purposes it *was* the real thing. In reality it was a child's toy. I asked Steve what he thought of the people who manufactured such toys. His opinion mirrored my own: 'I don't see the point. I do not see why anyone needs to produce an imitation or toy weapon that is so realistic because it does nothing but cause problems.'

As the head of Matrix had illustrated, the use of imitation weapons is problematic enough; but the gang member I had met the previous day didn't have his leg broken by a toy gun, and there was no getting away from the fact that of the fourteen weapons laid out in front of me, seven had the potential to kill. And of those seven, one firearm is responsible for 40 per cent of the gun crime in Liverpool. That weapon is the shotgun. The example in front of me was a sawn-off, and Steve explained to me why it is so popular. 'The controls around shotguns aren't as strong as controls around other weapons. And people can very easily and legally acquire shotgun cartridges.'

Shotguns might be easier to get hold of, but they're still incredibly dangerous weapons in the wrong hands; they might only take two rounds, but it only takes one round to kill somebody. Saw off the barrel and the gun becomes more manoeuvrable, easier to use at short range, simpler to conceal and the shot sprays more widely. One thing's for sure: the sawn-off I had in my hands certainly was no longer intended for clay-pigeon shooting.

From the evidence laid out in front of me, it was clear that the Matrix had had some success in removing guns from the streets; but from what the Noggsy crew had told me, guns are easily replaced. It appeared from what Steve Morris was showing me that the incidence of these weapons was on the increase. 'My message to people who think about using guns,' he confirmed, 'would be, you're not just *a* priority for Merseyside Police, you are *the* priority for Merseyside Police.'

There was a note of absolute determination in Steve's voice. I didn't doubt that he meant what he said.

Clearly gun crime in Liverpool is no flash in the pan. But things have not always been that way and I was determined to know where it all came from. The answer, as so often seems to be the case, is drugs.

As I said, the 1980s and 90s saw a massive increase in drug use across the country in general, and in Liverpool in particular. While junkies were becoming helplessly addicted to heroin, a whole different demographic was indulging in altogether more recreational drug use – or misuse, depending on your point of view. Ecstasy in particular became the drug of choice for the acid house and Madchester generations; the yuppies favoured cocaine. If you were a dealer, business was booming. In Liverpool there was one member of the criminal fraternity who thrived on this flourishing scene, a gangster with a serious reputation. His name was Stephen French; his enemies simply referred to him as the Devil.

French wasn't a dealer. Far from it. He earned his living in a very different way, targeting the dealers who were making such good money. Nowadays Stephen French has gone straight and is a successful legitimate businessman. I wanted to talk to him, to hear his reminiscences of his criminal days and to see if he could shed any light on just why there was an explosion of gun crime in the city.

Stephen French is a big man with a big reputation. He towers above me. In fact, he towers above pretty much anybody. Six foot five with a sharp suit, a shaved head and, despite the fact that he must be approaching fifty, barely an ounce of fat on him. We met in a high-class restaurant, a far cry from where I'm used to meeting gangsters, retired or otherwise. But French was no ordinary gangster. As a former child criminal, martial arts expert and bouncer from Toxteth – one of the most violent areas of inner-city Liverpool and scene of the notorious Toxteth riots – he became a master 'taxman'. In the world of crime 'taxing' is the violent extraction of money and drugs from dealers. It's a dangerous way to make a living, but a potentially lucrative one. When it came to taxation, Stephen French was one of the best.

As we sat in our comfortable chairs in a corner of this swanky restaurant looking out over the streets of Liverpool,

French explained to me how the proliferation of drugs in the 80s occurred. He chose his words carefully, making sure he incriminated no one, especially himself. 'An armed robbery would take place,' he told me. 'Maybe £20,000 was stolen between three individuals. Those three individuals would make a kitty of the £20,000. They'd go to Holland, and for £20,000 – allegedly, so I've been told – you could buy two kilos of cocaine. You buy those two kilos of cocaine and you get them into this country, they become worth £100,000.'

Buy for a dollar, sell for two. The rules of business apply in Toxteth just the same as they do in Threadneedle Street. There was a lot of money to be made, and the dealers were cash rich. It made them targets for the taxmen – and I'm not talking about the Inland Revenue. I asked French to describe what a taxman would do to a drug dealer in order to get his hands on the green.

He thought for a moment. 'There's the case of a friend of mine,' he said, 'who got eleven years for this offence. He burned the guy with an iron to get the guy to give up his stash, and he would iron the victim's genitals.'

Eye-watering stuff. I wondered how big the taxation business became in Liverpool. This clearly wasn't something French felt comfortable going into detail about. 'Money was made, Ross,' he told me cagily, 'and money was lost. It was a frivolous time. Money was made and money was lost, and that's all I'm prepared to say about that.'

I sensed, though, that it wasn't just about the money. I asked French if he was happy with himself at the time. His reply was surprisingly candid. 'The power that I felt was intoxicating. The feeling of invincibility that coursed through my body was real at that time. It's very easy to fake loving somebody. People can't fake fear. You can trust fear. You can understand fear. I can remember, to my detriment and to my shame, just wanting to be feared. Wanting to have that reputation. Wanting people to say, "There goes Frenchy. He's a bad man."'

From what I'd heard, he succeeded.

I was beginning to understand where it was that firearms came into the equation. If you're a dealer sitting on £100,000 and you're worried that someone with the reputation and physical presence of the Devil might be on his way to relieve you of it, chances are you're going to look for a way of swinging the odds a little more in your favour. I asked French the question plainly. 'Were dealers getting firearms because they were worried about people like you taxing them? Was it their way of defending themselves?'

'Excellent analysis,' French agreed. 'This is where I have to take some culpability in terms of the explosion of firearms on Merseyside. I don't take full responsibility, but the ten-stone weedy heroin dealer that's got forty grand under his bed and thinks the Devil's coming to get him – what's he going to do? It becomes an instant equalizer.'

Stephen French had admitted to me that he was personally involved in the emergence of guns in the city. Now, though, he is a reformed character, a man who has turned his back on crime and has a very different drum to bang. He told me what it was that had caused this turnaround. 'My lifelong friend Andrew John, shot dead in 1991. Four shots into the back. Stephen, my son, twenty-six years of age: shot twice, the second time almost fatally. When I went into the hospital to see him they had to put a pipe in his chest to drain the blood from his lungs and it's going into a bucket on the floor. To see your own offspring's claret collected on the floor is an experience to say the least.'

A conversation with Stephen French is an education in

itself. In the short time I was with him he had shown me both sides of the coin: he had explained how it was that gun use escalated in Liverpool, and he had described some of its devastating consequences. I respected him for his honesty; I also respected him for the way in which he is currently campaigning against gun crime. He spoke eloquently and passionately about his crusade. 'You have young men at home now, ten years of age, that will be hitting the streets in five years' time, ten years' time. They've uncles that are doing life, brothers that have been murdered, fathers who are murderers. They're desensitized. They're on the verge of being dehumanized. If we, as the elders of the village, don't find something to harness their energy, to give them focus, direction and purpose, mayhem's going to ensue.'

His words made sense. I felt that in the Norris Green crew I had already met the very youngsters he was talking about, and there was something reassuring about the fact that someone like this was taking an interest in their situation. For a man with his reputation, however, it is not an easy campaign. French recently collaborated on a book of his life – aptly titled *The Devil* – and as a result has been labelled a grass by certain members of the Liverpool criminal community. It's not an accusation I personally would like to throw at the feet of a man like Stephen French even if he has turned his back on crime. 'In my own community,' he told me, 'they took to daubing things on the wall about me. Stephen French is a police informer, Stephen French is a grass, Stephen French is a homosexual, Stephen French is this, that and the other. I've had seven attempts on my life so far. I've had prices on my head ranging from £5,000 to £30,000. The last attempt on my life was less than six weeks ago, when five shots were fired at me.'

I asked him why he thought there had been such a determined effort to kill him.

'My belief is,' he told me, 'that my anti-gun message is beginning to gather momentum.' It made sense that there might be people out there who wouldn't want that to happen, and I wondered how French – a man no stranger to violence – dealt with it. 'The temptation to revert to type and sort out those individuals that have had the effrontery to try to take my life is the hardest thing I have to resist. Because I could swat them like flies, mate. I could swat them like flies.'

Stephen French said these words to me with conviction. The man sitting in front of me was not bragging. He was not trying to prove to me how hard he was. He didn't have to. He was just telling me the truth.

I think French is probably right: young gangsters are more likely to listen to someone like him talking about gangs and gun violence than any number of police officers, politicians – or TV presenters for that matter. He's walking a dangerous line, though, and I wish him luck.

From what I had learned on my trip to Liverpool, it was clear that it had a substantial gang and gun problem. I wanted to learn more about the effect this had on the ordinary inhabitants of the city.

To start this process, I arranged to meet a young lad who had formerly been a member of one of the gangs of Liverpool. Our meeting place was on the outskirts of the city, and I wasn't quite sure what to expect when I got there. When we finally arrived, we were greeted by the sight of a bunch of lads wreaking havoc on motorbikes, quad bikes and four-by-fours. I don't really know what this display of bravado was supposed to prove, but we allowed ourselves to be impressed by their driving prowess before I sat down in the front of one of the four-by-fours to interview our man. Like the Norris Green crew, his hood was up and his face was covered. He didn't want to be identified on camera for reasons that would become obvious.

Our man was fourteen years old when he first joined a gang and freely admitted to me that he only did it because, in his own words, he was 'young and stupid'. He saw older kids with money and weed and wanted what they seemed to have. I asked him to give me an example of the sort of things he was asked to do as a fourteen-year-old new recruit. 'Mine shit [sell drugs], get guns, go and shoot people, anything like that.'

How easy was it for him to get his hands on weapons? How expensive were they?

'Cheap. You can get a shotgun for fifty quid. Go and blow someone's head off with it dead easy, can't you?'

He admitted to me that he personally had owned guns that he had bought illegally. Had he fired them, though?

'Not saying,' he replied warily.

I wanted to know who supplied guns to such young people. Were there specific gun dealers, just like there were drug dealers?

'Both. If you do drugs, you've got to have guns to protect yourself from getting robbed. If you're earning good money, people want a bit of it, don't they?' It was a more up-to-date echo of what Stephen French had told me.

From an early age the lad in the car with me had lived a dangerous life. 'But it felt good,' he explained. 'You're in a firm. You're all together. All for one and one for all, and all that.' What was it, then, that persuaded him to get out? 'Going to jail too many times.' He had been to prison four times, for stretches ranging from one to three years. For fear of being identified he wouldn't tell me how old he was, but suffice to say that I could look into his eyes and tell that he wasn't that old, which meant he had spent a lot of his young life behind bars.

Leaving a gang is a bold move. I asked him if he had found it difficult. 'It always is,' he replied. 'If you're looking at getting out, they'll be on you. They'll know that you're wanting to get out, somehow or other. They'll watch you, make sure that something goes missing so that you owe them money. Set you up so you're in debt to them for ever.'

Leave the gang under those circumstances, and you can get seriously hurt.

'You'll get shot,' he agreed. 'Dead easy. There's loads of shootings that you don't hear about. The papers don't print them.'

Had he personally been shot at? He answered without hesitation. 'Loads of times.'

Now that he had made a break from the world of gangs, I wanted to know what his opinion of the police was. I had some idea of what his answer would be because on the side of the vehicle in which we were sitting someone had written 'Fuck the Matrix' in the dirt. Sure enough, he spoke about them in less than glowing terms. 'Fuck them, horrible scumbags.' I wanted to know why he felt so much hatred towards them, and he seemed happy to tell me about the alleged police tactics that made him loathe them so much. 'They'll find weed on me,' he said, 'and won't nick me for it because I've been all right with them, but they'll nick my mate for it because he's been a knobhead with them.' It sounded to my ears like a minor thing – a bit like playground bickering – but it clearly rankled: this ex-gang member might have turned his back on crime but he had no respect for a single member of the police force. 'I hate them,' he reiterated. 'I always will.'

I knew from experience that leaving a gang, while not easy, was only the beginning. Some of the biggest problems come when the ex-gang member has to decide what he's going to replace that part of his life with. So, what now? I asked the lad in front of me. 'Just try and stay on the straight and narrow, keep away from it all. It's hard, though. You know what I mean?'

I certainly do, and I wish him luck. It's not going to be easy – he admitted to me off camera that he was constantly looking over his shoulder, half-expecting a violent reprisal to come at any minute. It sounded like a stressful way to live your life. I came away struck by how articulate and intelligent my interviewee was and I couldn't help thinking that he was like a lot of young men up and down the country: full of potential that is never going to be realized because of where he was brought up and the chances he never had.

But at least he's still alive. The same can't be said of everyone who has found themselves embroiled in the gang and gun problems of Liverpool. Liam Kelly was sixteen when, in June 2004, he was getting out of a car in the early hours of the morning. A masked gunman approached and shot him twice at point-blank range with a sawn-off shotgun. He was, at the time, the youngest victim of gun crime the city had ever seen, and his death shocked the whole of Liverpool. Liam was killed over a disputed debt of £200. A nineteen-year-old, Anthony Campbell, is serving twenty-three years for his murder; another suspect has never been traced.

I was to meet Liam's mum, to talk with the human face of the consequences of Liverpool's gun crime. Meeting the family members who are left behind after a violent killing is never easy, and talking to Liam Kelly's mother was no exception. She was a strong, feisty woman, but her despair at the loss of a son she loved so much was written plainly on her face and sounded clear in her voice. Mary Kelly made no attempt to portray her son as an angel. 'Liam was boyish,' she sighed. 'He was a proper boy. He was up to all kinds of mischief.'

But no one deserves to be shot for mischief. And no one deserves to be shot for £200 or for any sum of money for that matter. Liam's mum explained to me what had happened. 'It was coming up to his birthday,' she said. 'I gave him £200 out of his birthday money, not knowing that he was going to lend it to Anthony Campbell. Time went on and he never paid.' Liam heard that Anthony Campbell had come into some money and decided that the time really had come for him to pay up. He went round to Campbell's mother's house, but Anthony was not there. As he left the house, he picked up a bicycle in anger and threw it over his shoulder. It went through the Campbells' window. 'My son was killed for a bike going through the window,' Mary Kelly claimed. 'He was brutally killed for a bike.'

It was a shocking example of how violent mountains can be made from seemingly insignificant molehills. But the pain didn't stop there. I asked Mary Campbell if she had had any contact with the family of her son's killers. She sure had. Not long after the murder she came face to face with Campbell's mother. 'I'm sorry I ever let her go that day,' Mary told me, a look of absolute loathing on her face. 'If I ever come face to face with that woman again, I will not be held responsible for my actions.' Another of the murderer's family got away less lightly when Mary attacked her in a supermarket.

It would be easy to condemn Mary Kelly for allowing an already dreadful situation to escalate. But people react to grief in different ways, and I for one would not want to criticize anyone for the way they respond to the death of their child. It was clear, though, that what she was telling me was a graphic illustration of the way in which violence breeds violence.

It's very easy to tell people to forgive and forget; it's a lot less easier to do it.

Britain is lucky in that it doesn't have the *favelas* of Rio to contend with, or the corruption of Kenya. Our streets are not overrun with paramilitaries. How, then, should the UK deal with its gang problem? How should we stop the situation spiralling out of control? How do we stop the streets of Liverpool becoming like the streets of Compton, Los Angeles? I got together with the Merseyside police force to find out how they were approaching this very immediate problem.

The ex-gang member I had interviewed had accused the police of what at best could be considered harassment. But I had nothing to back what he was saying but his word. However, the last people I thought would admit to harassment were the police. It's often the case that they know which gang members are the perpetrators of gun crime, but they do not have enough evidence to arrest them. It's a difficult situation for the police: by the time they *have* enough evidence, a serious crime might have been committed. So what do they do?

The answer, at least one of them, surprised me. If you're the kind of person who is prepared to sell, carry or use guns, chances are you've got your finger in some less serious criminal pies. You're probably not going to be paying your road tax; you're probably going to have a tendency to shop-lift your milk from the supermarket; you're probably not going to have the right amount of air in the tyres of the car that you haven't insured. You might be signing on when you shouldn't; you might be on parole and have committed a minor infraction of your parole terms. I was told by the police themselves that their strategy is this: they approach their target and make it clear that they know the person in question is involved in gun crime. They tell their target that if they cease doing it now, they'll leave him alone. If he carries on, on the other hand, they'll find out if he's got insurance on his car; they'll find out if he's taxed it; they'll speak to the people in the supermarket and next time he steals something, they'll be on him. If the target already has a criminal record, as he most likely will have, he'll know that he'll be put away for even the smallest crime.

Some people may look at this as a legitimate way of keeping the heat up; others might contend that it's police harassment. My own opinion lands somewhere between the two. I can't make myself approve of it, but if it ultimately stops people being killed on the streets of the UK, then I guess it will have been for the best. It's an American system and I've seen it at work in St Louis and LA. It does stop crime but builds a resentment towards authority and sends criminality further underground.

There are other initiatives too – measures that I find rather more palatable. Staysafe is an initiative between the police and the local council aimed at keeping young people off the streets and away from the temptations of gang life. The initiative involves forty police officers hitting the streets of a particular area – most notably Croxteth and Norris Green – and picking up youngsters that they feel may be in danger. They are then brought back to the Staysafe headquarters to be interviewed by a team of social workers. The scheme is the brainchild of Chief Inspector Bill McWilliam who, alarmed when he went out on patrol by the sight of feral youngsters on the streets without any parental control, realized something had to be done to stop them going down the line of gang initiation. 'What we're doing,' he told me, 'is lawful, but it's also needed – not just to protect young people, which is the main aim of this, but also to send out a strong message to criminals, a strong message to those who want to engage in antisocial behaviour that it's not going to be tolerated; but also a strong message to parents that we need their help and support, and for them to engage with us.'

What Bill was describing to me was a holistic approach to the problem of gang crime. I went out with one of his units to see how they operated. It didn't take long for us to come across a young kid who had been drinking. He was ushered into a police van and taken back to the Staysafe HQ. There he was sat down and spoken to by a team of social workers.

The lad fitted the demographic of the majority of people who are picked up by Staysafe, most of whom are between ten and sixteen years of age, and many of whom have been drinking. The initiative has the ability to take youngsters into care, but so far they have yet to use that power. The purpose of Staysafe is rather different. I asked Jimmy Clarke, the leading social worker involved, to explain just what it was they were trying to achieve. 'It's inappropriate,' he told me, 'for a child to be walking through a park drunk. It's inappropriate for a child to be running across the road without adult authority. It's inappropriate for a child to be walking down the road with a knife and no one saying, "That's stupid." What we're saying is, "It's inappropriate and we give a damn." Maybe not enough adults say we care enough to say, "Stop, we give a damn."'

I wondered if they ever came across resistance from parents who resented this interference in the way they brought up their children.

'One parent came to us and said, "Why have you picked up my nine-year-old for running across the road?" One of the police officers said, "Would you rather we turned up with a box?"' This is a low-level way – it won't change the world overnight – of social services, the police and the Youth Offending Service saying we care enough to say this is inappropriate; you're unsafe; stop it. Sometimes young people don't get that instant consequence which stops them escalating their behaviour up towards antisocial behaviour, criminality and gun crime.'

I thought back to the Norris Green crew and the ex-gang member I had interviewed. They had a total disregard for authority and I wondered if that was an issue for the Staysafe team.

'For those kids that escalate towards gun and gang crime,' Jimmy told me, 'I think what you've got to look at is how the mother and father act as role models. If your mother or father is a drug or alcohol misuser, you'd never, ever build up a model of adult authority being useful to you. That's why nowadays, I think, you see more and more violence by kids towards adults, because some of these kids never understood what adults bring to the table apart from drug misuse and alcohol misuse.'

I walked away from Staysafe with a vague sense of optimism. Some people might think that flooding the streets with police in order to nick a few kids who've had too much to drink is a bit like breaking a butterfly on a wheel. I had a very different impression. These people were trying to nip the problem in the bud. They were trying to show young people at risk of becoming gang members that there were adults out there who cared about them and that authority was not something to be despised or disregarded.

It's difficult to measure the success or otherwise of a scheme like this. The police claim that antisocial behaviour is down 21 per cent in Staysafe areas, but that could be due to any number of reasons. What is beyond question, though, is that making parents aware of the activities of their kids and instilling in those kids a sense of respect for authority is a step in the right direction. At the time of writing the scheme is attracting national attention, and I would like to think that its good work will continue to thrive.

The police of Liverpool are obviously making a big push to stop youngsters from entering gangs. But for some of them it's too late, as the inter-gang warfare between Norris Green and Croxteth made perfectly clear. I had hooked up with the Noggsy lads to hear what they had to say. The Croccy Crew were being a little more camera shy. Eventually, however, towards the end of my stay, we got word that they were prepared to talk to us and give their side of the story.

We met in a park in Croxteth. There were seven of them, not including the dog that one of them kept on a short leash. What was most noticeable about them, however, was the fact that, to my eye, there was absolutely nothing to distinguish these young men from the ones I had interviewed over in Norris Green. They wore the same regulation black clothes, the same label, and to a man they had their hoods up and their faces covered in the same way. I had no doubt that the similarities didn't end there. I'd been told that the Croccy Crew had all gone to the same school as the Norris Green lot; it wouldn't have been a huge leap of intuition to suggest that their home lives weren't a whole lot different either. And yet, from talking to them, it was clear that the hatred that the Norris Green gang had expressed towards Croxteth was fully reciprocated. And, if anything, these lads were more aggressive towards me.

They stood in a line, shifting edgily from foot to foot as if they were nervous about being caught talking to me. I asked them what it was like living in this part of town. 'Rough,' one of them told me. 'Good,' another shouted out. 'Like a ghost town after ten,' a third suggested.

With a giggle, one of them made me an offer. 'Come round, stay for a while.' A few others laughed at his joke. 'This place shits on Afghanistan.'

I held my tongue.

I wanted to hear what the Croccy Crew had to say about the violence on the street. Do people carry guns?

'Obviously!' a voice called out. 'People get shot dead.' Another little giggle.

I'd heard from other people during my stay how easy it was to get a gun in Liverpool. What did these lads have to say about it? 'Depends who you are,' one of them told me. And on what you're after – a shotgun's easier to get than a nine-millimetre pistol, just as I'd heard elsewhere.

I wondered if it was possible to hire guns. The answer was a unanimous no. 'No one hires nothing out of no one. They're not going to get it back – as soon as you use it, you've got to buy it anyway.'

Their responses to my questions were shirty and bitty. But what struck me was how conversant they were with gun culture – the way they talked about weapons with complete knowledge and confidence. I had no doubt that, despite their playful attitude towards me, I at least wasn't being bullshitted in this respect – these guys knew *where* to get guns, they knew *how* to get guns and they knew what to do with them once they were in their possession.

I wanted to know a bit more about their situation, about what they did with their time. None of them had jobs, they told me. I asked them how easy it would be to get one. 'Not easy at all. We're not even allowed on the fucking dole because it's in Norris Green.'

Having spoken to the Norris Green crew, I could see why that might be a problem. So what exactly did they think of the rival gang? 'Scumbags. Dogs. Rapists. Mongrels.' They trotted off a list of abuse, but gave no inkling as to *why* they thought that way. And so I asked them. Their response was as unenlightening as when I had asked the Norris Green gang the same question. 'They're scumbags. They rape girls. They rape our women.' These were pretty hardcore accusations. The malice these young men felt towards their enemies positively dripped from them. The dog seemed to feel it too. All of a sudden it went wild, jumping up at some of the members of the gang, snarling and barking. It had to be pulled back sharply by his handler and kicked into submission. The sudden display of aggression didn't seem to worry the lads too much, and I had the impression that it was a pretty regular occurrence. I was glad the dog was on a short leash.

The gang members, on the other hand, were free to run wild – and that's just what they did. Having all been to the same school, the Croxteth gang admitted that they could recognize the Norris Green crew by sight. What happened, I asked them, if one of them dared to come across the border into Croxteth? 'They're fucked. They get dealt with, don't they?'

What exactly did they mean by that?

'What do *you* think it means?' one of them asked me evasively.

So far the gang had done a very good job of telling me how much they hated Norris Green. But they *still* hadn't told me why. What's the beef about? I asked them again. Why is there so much loathing and violence between them? Why do they want to kill each other?

A brief pause. 'We're not prepared to tell you,' one of them said, and the others murmured their agreement. I couldn't help feeling that it wasn't so much a case of not being prepared to tell me as of not knowing.

I started to tell them that to my untrained eye there wasn't anything to distinguish them from the Norris Green gang members I had met. They agreed. 'It's just the way they act,' one of them said vaguely. But before I could ask him to expand on that, we heard shouts. The police had arrived. Whether they had been tipped off that the Croccy Crew were all in one place or it was just a random patrol, I couldn't say. The gang weren't going to hang around to find out. 'Go!' someone shouted. 'Go! Go!'

Like birds dispersing at the sound of gunshot, the lads disappeared. If I wanted to find out more about them, I was going to be disappointed. That was the last we saw of the Croccy Crew.

It was time to go home, and I left the city with mixed feelings. I'd enjoyed my stay there, and off camera had made some good friends – I revelled in the company of the many intelligent, witty Liverpudlians I had met. But at the same time I had learned some alarming truths about the reality of life for some of our young people today. Having talked to some of the Liverpool gangs, I saw that there was a very different side to the city, an underbelly of disenfranchisement, unemployment, gun crime and inter-group hatred.

It would be a misrepresentation to claim that Liverpool

is overrun by gangs, and to forget the many positives of this wonderful town. The unfortunate truth, however, is that parts of Liverpool aren't that much different to many other parts of the country, where gun crime and feral behaviour by young gang members is an ever-present issue. In Liverpool it's more concentrated than it is in, say, London or Birmingham, and the existence of an active port means it's easier to get hold of contraband such as drugs and illegal firearms. But it would be a mistake to say that this is just Liverpool's problem. A dangerous mistake.

Is this the thin end of the wedge? Are we in the UK poised on the brink of an explosion of gang and gun crime that will plunge us into a situation like that which I had seen on the streets of LA or Colombia? It would be easy for me glibly to say that we are. It would also be disingenuous because the truth is that I don't know. Nobody knows. The seeds have been sown, of that there can be no doubt, but there are systems and schemes in place to keep crime under control. Some of them, like Staysafe, are a definite step in the right direction; others, like the targeting of known gun criminals for petty misdemeanours, raise serious questions about personal liberty and what freedoms we are prepared to forgo to stop the proliferation of gang crime on our streets.

What does, however, seem to me to be the case is that the people involved in gang crime are generally getting younger. The gang members I met in Liverpool were cagey about revealing their ages to me for fear of identifying themselves, but it was perfectly clear that they were little more than teenagers. This is a worrying development. In the *favelas* of Rio I observed a similar thing. Whereas the gang elders used to be seventeen or eighteen, now they're thirteen or fourteen. If we're heading in the same direction, it is truly something to be concerned about.

Operation Trident, the Metropolitan Police's initiative to combat gun crime in London's black community, has noticed a similar trend with regard to the age of the people they are targeting. I think it is true to say that black-on-black gang violence has a higher place in the public consciousness than, say, the gang violence between Croxteth and Norris Green. But during my time with the Liverpool gangs I would have to say that I didn't see a single non-white face. It brought home to me one unavoidable fact. We are at risk of dismissing gang culture in the UK, of pretending that it's a problem restricted to ethnic minorities and localized communities.

It isn't. The murder of Rhys Jones tells us that, as does the ease with which working-class white kids all over the country can – and do – get hold of deadly firearms. Gang membership will increase when life is hard, regardless. According to what you read in the papers, we are set for a global recession and, as is always the case, it is the underclass that will be affected first. Gangs and guns in the UK are not a black problem. They're not a white problem either.

They're a social problem.

They're a youth problem.

They're *our* problem.

Acknowledgements

I would like to thank:

Lord Waheed Alli, Michael Foster, Clive Tulloh and Matt Bennett, Tom Watson, Wendy Banks and everyone at Tiger Aspect. Thanks to Andrew O'Connell and Richard Woolfe from Sky. The researchers, directors and crews. Adam Parfitt – without him this book wouldn't have been written.

Thanks to my editor, Katy Follain, Catherine Duncan and everyone at Penguin.

I would like to thank all the contributors – without them there would be no book.

My Mum is the last person I have to mention – if I don't, I won't get any Christmas dinner this year!